The

90-DAY
BIBLE
READING

DEVOTIONAL

for Men

The
90-DAY
BIBLE
READING

DEVOTIONAL

for Men

Glenn Hascall

BARBOUR
PUBLISHING

ISBN 978-1-63609-666-7

Published by Barbour Publishing, Inc., 1810 Barbour Drive, Uhrichsville, Ohio 44683, www.barbourbooks.com

Our mission is to inspire the world with the life-changing message of the Bible.

Printed in China.

INTRODUCTION

Welcome to *The 90-Day Bible Reading Devotional for Men*, a place where you can commune with God and His Word, Jesus Christ and the Holy Spirit. This is your entry to a quiet time of prayer, reading, and reflection, a way of discovering what God is speaking directly into your life. As you hear from Him, you'll better know how to think, what to say, where to go, and what to do.

This book contains three topical 30-day Bible reading plans:

- Getting to Know God
- Knowing Jesus Better
- Growing in Your Faith

Each of the daily entries covers a specific topic and includes a scripture reading, two or three questions to contemplate, and a related devotional. Every entry concludes with a prayer starter to help you put what you've learned into practice.

But we suggest you also pray *before* beginning each day's study. Ask for the Holy Spirit's illumination. Make it your intention to listen to what God is saying through His Word. Then absorb the Bible passage for that day. Afterward, before looking at any commentary or considering that day's questions, mark the verse or passage that specifically speaks to you in this place and time—whether or not you understand why.

Then go on to the questions for that day. Reflect on each one. Consider the question that resonates most—or the verse you have already marked—and see what more God may reveal. The point is to follow where God leads. At the end of your reflection time, read the devotional and pray the prayer starter, remembering to ask God to solidify His truth in your heart, soul, and life.

Here is an opportunity to dig deeper into God's written truth, in the interest of informing your own thoughts, purpose, dreams, and life. The Lord is happy to reveal His ways to all who will seek Him in truth.

All Scripture is inspired by God and is useful to teach us what is true and to make us realize what is wrong in our lives. It corrects us when we are wrong and teaches us to do what is right.

2 TIMOTHY 3:16 NLT

30 DAYS OF BIBLE READINGS
FOR GETTING TO KNOW GOD

This is what the LORD says. . . "Those who wish to boast should
boast in this alone: that they truly know me and understand
that I am the LORD who demonstrates unfailing love."
JEREMIAH 9:23–24 NLT

Is God mysterious? You might believe that He can't really be known. On the other hand, some people who believe this don't spend much time reading the Bible. They might be more interested in the latest biography or mystery.

This book features three 30-day Bible reading plans. This first plan concentrates on God—Father, Son, and Holy Spirit—and what you can know about Him. A month will not be enough to even scratch the surface of the topic, but it will help to prove that God is worth knowing.

Spend some time reading the Bible every day. We all have our own thoughts about God, but let the Bible be your standard. Read it first and let God show you what He wants you to know. He created you and wants you to know Him. Start with creation and follow the road to relationship.

Commit yourself to Bible study for the next thirty days and see how God chooses to make Himself known to you.

Day 1
GOD THE CREATOR

Read Genesis 1:1–2:3

*In the beginning God created the heaven and the
earth. And the earth was without form, and void;
and darkness was upon the face of the deep. And the
Spirit of God moved upon the face of the waters.*

GENESIS 1:1–2 KJV

Questions to Consider

- The Spirit of God hovered over the darkness (Genesis 1:2), the unknown, looking to create order. What does this tell you about God? What might this mean to you personally?

- What God speaks comes into being; it is created. How do your words "create" things? What are you bringing into being with your words?

- What does it mean to you to know you have been created in the image of God? How can you reflect Him in your daily life?

Today's Devotional

Words have unexpected power—profound in their ability to affirm or destroy. They create worlds of chaos or worlds that welcome the wandering. God created something impressive with His words, and His example perfects a strategy for men to use.

Your words can create something that welcomes family and friends to a better, safer place, or they can make them feel unsafe.

It may be time for an evaluation of your "word creations." Do those who care about you most see creation words that demonstrate love and affirmation, or do they see something less creative? More destructive?

You have options. You get to make something positive or negative—one word at a time. Speak, write, or sing the words that flood your heart. These words will reveal what's really there. You are creating something with the words that spill from your lips. What are you creating? Is it what you need to create?

Consider this: after God had created everything, He took time to look it over, "and he saw that it was very good!" (Genesis 1:31 NLT).

Prayer

I was made in Your image, God. You brought beauty into my world. When others spoke words of betrayal, You spoke life. When some spoke words of pain, You spoke healing. Help me today do the same.

Day 2
GOD THE SUSTAINER

Read Genesis 2:4–24

The LORD God had planted a garden in the east, in Eden; and there he put the man he had formed. The LORD God made all kinds of trees grow out of the ground— trees that were pleasing to the eye and good for food.
GENESIS 2:8–9 NIV

Questions to Consider

- To *sustain* means to support, to continue to hold up without fail. What comes to your mind knowing that God has created all things to hold you up—including the earth beneath your feet—and continues to do so in your life today?

- God formed the earthly body of Adam (meaning "earth") from the soil but formed Eve (meaning "life"), his equal partner, not from the earth or the animal kingdom but from the rib of man himself. What does this tell you about God as a *creative* sustainer?

Today's Devotional

Babies are born. It's a fact, and parents take home new life every day from hospitals throughout the world. They are charged with the responsibility of caring for (sustaining) that young child.

For many first-time parents this seems like someone made a mistake. They are frightened. How can they be responsible for a new life? They have never had to do that before. Will they break the baby? The care required seems overwhelming.

God understands. He created the earth and then He took responsibility for the care of it every day from that point on. You can raise children until they are eighteen and then they might leave to take care of themselves—but the earth? It requires God's attention every single day. From trees to fish, animals to plants, day to night, God makes sure it all happens just right. He has. He does. He will.

Scripture provides many proofs that God doesn't ask you to do something He won't do Himself. He has always been creatively responsible. He never starts any project He won't see through to the end.

Prayer

You never forget I exist, Father. You stay near and keep providing everything I need to exist. May my own family see that I'm willing to pay attention to their needs every day.

Day 3
GOD OF PROMISES

Read Genesis 15

After these things the word of the Lord came unto Abram in a vision, saying, Fear not, Abram: I am thy shield, and thy exceeding great reward.
Genesis 15:1 kjv

Questions to Consider

- God talked to Abram in a vision. In what ways has God spoken to you?

- God told Abram not to fear before the man would even admit he was worried. What does this suggest to you?

- On one side are God's promises that are beyond a beginning, end, or distance. On the other, your trust and reliance on the vastness of these things. Can you think of a promise from God for which He is waiting for you to choose trust as your option of choice?

Today's Devotional

You've seen babies soon after they are born, and you've attended funerals of those whose lives have ended. This is an accessible view of beginning and end. You know how far it is from your home to the home of a friend. That's distance.

What you're not able to comprehend is where the universe begins and ends or how to measure God's existence.

If you could answer those questions precisely, you could clearly know the way in which God protects and rewards His own. But since such knowledge is "too wonderful" for us (Psalm 139:6 KJV), we simply accept by faith what we read in scripture and observe in our own lives. We know enough of God's protection and rewards to realize that He knows, accepts, and loves us.

There is no need for fear. Anxiety shouldn't get an invitation. Worry is not on the guest list. When you understand just how personal God's care is, you can dig deeper into the other important aspects of life—His and yours. It's certainly worth the investment of these thirty days. The dividends will be eternal.

Prayer

You are God. You are Lord. You are holy and You protect me. I do not know when or how Your protection has rescued me, but it means everything to me that You, the Creator of all, notice me and keep me safe.

Day 4
GOD OF HOLINESS

Read Exodus 3

"Do not come any closer," the LORD warned. "Take off your sandals, for you are standing on holy ground."
EXODUS 3:5 NLT

Questions to Consider

- When was the last time you "took off your sandals" when meeting with God in a demonstration of respect and reverence for His holiness?

- In what ways do you pause in God's presence, preparing every part of you—mind, body, heart, spirit, and soul—for a heavenly meeting, knowing your imperfection will be in the presence of God's perfection?

- How does your acknowledgment of God's holiness affect you—before, during, and after prayer?

Today's Devotional

God wants to be your friend. Knowing this might tempt you to alter the way you approach Him. It might make sense to treat Him like a coworker, a buddy from the gym, or a really good neighbor. This kind of response is far too casual for the God who created you, sustains your life, and prepares a future for you.

The respect Moses showed is an exceptional example of how God desires to be approached. Yes, be bold, brave, and confident in meeting with God, but refuse to treat Him as common. God set the tone for this unexpected meeting with Moses. He essentially told the man to stay where he was and take off his shoes because there was nothing common about this meeting.

When Moses understood the importance of this conversation, it altered the trajectory of his future. He was in the vicinity of eighty years of age and probably not looking for a new career path. But there was God—in a burning bush—giving new directions that challenged Moses' willingness. You have to wonder if Moses would have been less willing if he'd viewed this encounter as a casual, insignificant experience.

Prayer

I don't want to treat You as something less than You are, God. Teach me to be respectful and show You the honor You deserve. You want me to come to You, but You also want me to realize You're so much more than one of the guys.

Day 5
GOD THE VICTOR

Read Exodus 15:1–21

*The LORD is my strength and song, and he is become
my salvation: he is my God, and I will prepare him an
habitation; my father's God, and I will exalt him.*
EXODUS 15:2 KJV

Questions to Consider

- After miraculously escaping the Egyptian pharaoh and
  his army, God's people sang a song of victory, saying the
  Lord, their strength and their song, had become their
  salvation. On what occasion(s) have you come out of a
  personal battle unscathed and recognized God's help in
  word or song?

- What do you need to do today to tap into God's strength,
  assured that with Him, you need fear no enemy or flood,
  and will, in the end, find firm footing on dry land?

Today's Devotional

Today's verse doesn't describe history's first musical, but it
may feel that way. It's not often that people burst into spon-
taneous song about, well, anything.

Then again, how often have you witnessed something

as powerful as the rescue of what was likely more than a million people? And this rescue was completed in a way that far exceeded anything the people had ever seen—a dry path in the middle of the sea, a wall of water on either side. The Israelites made it through, but the enemy did not. That kind of thing doesn't happen every day. The God who oversaw this was powerful enough to assure the outcome of mankind's worst days.

The joy you feel should find an outlet. God doesn't demand that you sing, but He does enjoy hearing it. And if you're absolutely not a singer, any joyful noise will do.

The plans God passes along to the willing have never failed. Yes, opposition exists and it can seem oppressive—but when the plan is God's and not just yours, the victory is assured. And that's a perfect time to proclaim God's victory. He continues to do amazing things.

Prayer

You win, Father. That's not a declaration of personal loss but an admission of a victory I can't claim on my own. You do what I can't and orchestrate outcomes in ways I never saw coming. You are the winner. Help me to be bold enough to say so.

Day 6
GOD OF PURITY

Read Exodus 20

Moses said to the people, "Do not be afraid. God has come to test you, so that the fear of God will be with you to keep you from sinning."
EXODUS 20:20 NIV

Questions to Consider

- Why do you think God wrote these Ten Commandments, which clearly point out His purity and humankind's impurity?

- The first four commandments are about your relationship with God, and the rest about your relationship with others. What are you doing well? Where do you fall short?

- What might God be pinpointing for you in today's reading? What do you need to confess to draw nearer to Him?

Today's Devotional

The verdict is in. You're a sinner. You break God's laws. Romans 3:23 couldn't be any clearer: "all have sinned and fall short of the glory of God" (NIV). Not just a few or even many. *All* is inclusive language that makes it clear no one has ever kept every one of God's laws.

Exodus 20 is a showcase of the more common laws people break. But the God who gave us these laws never broke them. He doesn't covet, steal, or kill. He made life and sustains it, and makes new life available to all who break His law. That's every human being.

If you honor and respect God, you will be less likely to want to break His law—even though you will still fail from time to time.

Jesus simplified things when He said that those who follow God should love Him first and then love everyone else. The ten commands found in Exodus 20 can be summed up by loving God and then loving people.

The purity of God changes lives. It welcomes men like you to make the bold choice for purity yourself.

Prayer

Lord, I want to walk in purity. Please keep my footsteps aligned with Yours. When I'm walking consistently with You, my heart will be clean. Guide me today and every day.

Day 7
GOD OF GLORY

Read Exodus 33:7–23

*"If it is true that you look favorably on me, let me
know your ways so I may understand you more
fully and continue to enjoy your favor."*
EXODUS 33:13 NLT

Questions to Consider

- Moses asked to see God's glory but could not see God's
  face and live. So God protected Moses by putting him
  in a cleft of rock, then covering the man with His hand
  as He went by. Moses was allowed to see God's back but
  not His face. What does this tell you about the love and
  care God has for His people?

- In what ways do you experience God's glory in nature?
  In the rest of His creation? In your life?

Today's Devotional

God is a God of incomparable glory. There's no one like
Him. He has no peer. No equal.

This God led Moses to leave his retirement home in
the wilderness and lead the Israelites out of Egypt on their
way to a land the Lord had promised to give them. Moses

had witnessed the burning bush. He'd heard God's voice. And he'd seen miracles that could only be attributed to this really big God.

Exodus 33 describes a time when God did something unusual. No human could actually see God and not be overwhelmed to the point of death. Yet Moses *wanted* to see God. While not a perfect comparison, you might think of this event as arriving late for a photo opportunity. Moses was only allowed to see God after He'd passed by.

Who had Moses known who had been blessed this way? Who would understand? No one. Why would God be so kind as to bless him this way?

Moses stood in the literal glory of God. If you were in such a situation, you might imagine all your insecurities being exposed or your sin and poor choices being highlighted. Running away might seem like a great option. Yet Moses stayed and witnessed God's glory. Moses witnessed God's love.

Prayer

God, I thank You for the evidence of Your glory that I see in creation. Help me to speak gratitude for the glory I see now, and to anticipate the fuller glory I'll experience in Your presence in eternity.

Day 8
GOD OF BLESSING

Read Deuteronomy 28

If thou shalt hearken diligently unto the voice of the LORD thy God, to observe and to do all his commandments which I command thee this day, that the LORD thy God will set thee on high above all nations of the earth.
DEUTERONOMY 28:1 KJV

Questions to Consider

- God says that if you listen to and obey His voice, He will shower you with a myriad of blessings that will overtake you. When have you felt God's blessings showering you as a result of your listening to His voice?

- God wants you to continue following His path, not turning aside to go another way. What spiritual practice have you found that keeps you in His way? How well are you sticking with that practice? What blessings do you lose when you stray from His way?

Today's Devotional

When you think of the word *voice,* it links to a sound. That sound comes from an individual and this sound forms words that have meaning. The voice you hear is unique and distinctive. You can learn to identify who's speaking before you see that person—simply because you recognize his or her voice.

It's not common for God to speak audibly to people. It is far more common for people to hear God's voice through the words written in the Bible. They exist to clarify God's thoughts. They are linked to receiving God's commands. They are filled with words that invite courage and boldness. The more you read the Word, the more you will recognize who's speaking.

God gives promises to those who listen to His voice. He wants active listeners—which translates to active *readers* of His Word. He wants those active readers to hear His words, understand their meaning, and then do what He asks.

Maybe you've heard God's voice as you've read His words at the suggestion of this book. Keep reading. Keep listening. Keep praying. Keep discovering blessing.

Prayer

There are words You want me to hear with my eyes, Father. Keep speaking to me through what I read. Help me understand and obey as I trust and follow.

Day 9
GOD OF JUDGMENT

Read Judges 10:6–16

*Because the Israelites forsook the LORD and no
longer served him, he became angry with them.*
JUDGES 10:6–7 NIV

Questions to Consider

- In what ways have you forsaken God by worshipping anything other than Him?

- When was the last time you prayed to God for help? Why would we ever hesitate to request His aid?

- In what ways, in His mercy and compassion, has God rescued you from yourself? In what ways do you think your troubles became His?

Today's Devotional

They said they would follow God. They once agreed to be set apart for His use. They began an amazing quest, yet they set aside their unique place, turned in any direction that pleased them, and walked away from the gift of compassion. They walked away from the God who delights in demonstrating mercy, the God who called them back and received the silent treatment, and the God who wanted to give them purpose while their actions said, "No thanks!"

When you choose to disobey God you choose to sin. That's the simple truth. The people of Israel watched God rescue them from slavery, perform miracle after miracle, feed them in the wilderness and provide a land for them to live in. It wasn't enough. They chose sin as their full-time companion and in the end God had enough.

If that sounds impulsive and harsh you should know that mercy is His preferred option. His kindness is the start of a turnaround for many people. When mercy, kindness, and love are ignored God sends justice. Given enough time the people would recognize error, turn from it, and discover a restored friendship with God—not much different than the way a timeout changed the attitude of the young boy you once were.

Prayer

Help me recognize Your mercy, kindness, and love as a reminder to come back to You, Lord. I don't want to wait for a heavier form of correction.

Day 10
GOD THE UNRIVALED

Read 1 Kings 18:16–46

Immediately the fire of the LORD flashed down from heaven and burned up the young bull, the wood, the stones, and the dust. It even licked up all the water in the trench! And when all the people saw it, they fell face down on the ground and cried out, "The LORD—he is God! Yes, the LORD is God!"

I KINGS 18:38–39 NLT

Questions to Consider

- What false gods are vying for your personal attention? What might you need to do to rebuild your altar to the Lord?

- God—the one who has power over fire, water, clouds, and rain—desires the entire heart, mind, body, soul, and spirit of His people. What can you do to show Him you are wholly His?

- How does it feel knowing you are the son of the unrivaled God?

Today's Devotional

It was something much more important than a televised contest pitting human against human. Elijah was on a mountain.

He stood for God and God was with him. Everyone else? These were the people of the great rejection. They believed two things: 1) God was not real, and 2) a non-god was. Elijah let them put their theory to the test.

God was the only one who showed up. He was the only one who could. God has no rival who is in any way equal to Him. When Satan attempts to rival God he can't do it directly. Satan attacks the people God loves. So the God who can't be beaten promised to stay close to those who may find themselves in the bullseye of trouble.

And when this unrivaled God shows up do not fail to speak up and say what everyone should, "The LORD—he is God! Yes, the LORD is God!"

Prayer

There is absolutely no one like You, God. No one can challenge You or win against You. Help me to remember that when my days of trouble come.

Day 11
GOD OF MAJESTY

Read Psalm 8

Thou madest him to have dominion over the works of thy hands; thou hast put all things under his feet.
PSALM 8:6 KJV

Questions to Consider

- When did you last consider the majesty of God and the awesome works of His creation that surround you every day?

- How does it alter your thinking to know that although you are just a speck in God's universe you are also His child?

- What things has God put into your hands and under your feet? How is His majesty reflected in these things, large and small?

Today's Devotional

When the James Webb Space Telescope started sending pictures back to this big blue marble they were stunning in clarity and presented scientists with answers to a mystery. It seems the universe is not disorderly like they had originally thought. They didn't witness the chaos they expected. It was as if what they witnessed showed incredible order.

The God of majesty wasn't surprised by the news. He didn't even need a telescope to see it. And this same God who made everything—including all the things you'll never see in the vastness of space—also made you. He has a plan for you. There's a purpose for you. God will help—you.

Let Him bring order to the chaos that rages within your heart, soul, mind, and body. He will give you insight into the things He is anxious to see you do.

This God does not need a telescope to see His creation. He doesn't need a microscope to zoom in on the details. He doesn't need a stethoscope to check the condition of your heart.

He already has a perfect view and knowledge of His own. And God is just waiting for your response to Him. As a human being, you're at the top of His creation—where it's easiest to reach out and touch Him.

Prayer

Thank You for making me part of Your plan, Father. Everything You've created can make me feel small. . .but Your personal care shows that Your majesty has come to my house.

Day 12
GOD OF LIFE

Read Psalm 16

You will show me the way of life, granting me the joy of your presence and the pleasures of living with you forever.
PSALM 16:11 NLT

Questions to Consider

- Is your soul speaking to the Lord today?

- When was the last time you asked God for advice; allowed Him to speak to your heart in the night; set Him at your right hand, knowing that with Him there, you need not worry about anything because He is your protector in this great quest?

- In what ways have you allowed God to show you the path of life and, in so doing, found joy in His presence and pleasure in choosing eternal life with Him?

Today's Devotional

Life! You get to live it, experience it, and share it. There is a way to do all of this and find joy in the doing. There is a forever life that comes after your body stops working and that life is spent in the presence of God. There is also new life that fits somewhere between the moment you are born and the moment your current life ends. This new life bridges the gap between your old life and heaven. In the end, you get God and everything God has waiting for you.

Nothing exists without God. Nothing is sustained without Him. Nothing can survive without Him. God knows how to live this life, and He can teach you if you will allow it. And why wouldn't you?

There is little joy in simply existing, which is why you should remember that you were made for more. Learning about this new way of life can enhance your satisfaction more than anything you can earn, buy, or make on your own. If life were a cell phone, you couldn't do better than having God as your primary contact. If life were a sports car, He'd be your fuel. If life is what it is—and it is—God is your everything. Make Him your primary pursuit.

Prayer

Give me life, Lord, Your life. Give me joy. Show me Your way. Help me navigate this quest on the path of new life.

Day 13
GOD OF SUPREMACY

Read Psalm 19

In the heavens God has pitched a tent for the sun. . . .
It rises at one end of the heavens and makes its circuit
to the other; nothing is deprived of its warmth.
PSALM 19:4, 6 NIV

Questions to Consider

- What have you witnessed in God's creation that tells you of His overwhelming supremacy over all of nature?

- In what ways does God reveal Himself and His power in your soul, thoughts, heart, and spirit?

- In what ways have you *not* given God free rein in your life. Are all of your words, your actions, your thoughts, your heart, your soul, and your spirit pleasing to Him, the ruler of all?

Today's Devotional

So God can pitch a tent for the sun. If the sun is more than 100 times larger than earth, and the earth is much bigger than your country, and your country is bigger than your town, and your town is bigger than your house, and your house is bigger than you are, then might it be safe to say that God is bigger than all?

As supreme as God is and as many things as He takes care of, this same God is dialed completely into a friendship with you. There is no reason to treat Him with suspicion, distrust, or fear. He doesn't need anything you have in order to survive, though you need all of Him. God made sure the earth would have equal access to the brilliance of the sun. He also made sure everyone would have equal access to the brilliance of His Son. No one else is bigger. No one can ever be better. God is better than all.

Supremacy is one more perfect way to describe Him.

Prayer

You are over all, God. You are in all and above all. You made all and sustain all. All there is exists because You spoke. I am here because once upon a time You called my name. Thank You.

Day 14
GOD THE SHEPHERD

Read Psalm 23

Yea, though I walk through the valley of the shadow of death, I will fear no evil: for thou art with me; thy rod and thy staff they comfort me.
PSALM 23:4 KJV

Questions to Consider

- As you imagine God as your shepherd—the one who provides for you, gives you rest, stills your spirit, restores your soul, comforts you, guards you, and guides you—which of His provisions means the most to you? Why?

- What dark valley might you be walking through right now? What light is God shining into your fearful moments?

- How would your life change if you were conscious every moment that God the Shepherd is walking with you, leading you, and covering you?

Today's Devotional

Psalm 23 may seem like a sampler pack of God's blessings. It's true—He doesn't just offer one thing, but *all* good things. This psalm describes life as you live it: hurried, harried, fearful, lost, and lacking courage.

Every day you will experience moments that have no discernible road map. It all seems overwhelming and chaotic. An honest evaluation leads to the conclusion that God is a shepherd to your tendency to be a lost sheep. He is good. He is kind. He knows the best way to go. And sometimes the best way is through dark valleys with shadows and fear. His design isn't to lead you *to* those things but *through* them.

If you walk through storms, God can calm them. If you walk through dark valleys, He can light your way. If you are simply overwhelmed by the unknown, He will remind you who He is. And He is all you need.

Prayer

I have been all of the things You are not, Father. You are everything I need. May I stay close enough to You that I can learn to walk in Your steps, engage with Your kindness, and love with the same love I receive from You.

Day 15
GOD OF PEACE

Read Psalm 29

The LORD gives his people strength.
The LORD blesses them with peace.
PSALM 29:11 NLT

Questions to Consider

- In what ways do you offer praise and worship to God before, during, and after the storms in your life? How might worshipping God *before* the storm help you endure it, to find peace in the midst of chaos?

- What comfort do you find by knowing God is more powerful than any storm you could encounter—that even in the downpour of life, He is still on the throne and always will be?

- Where and in what situation are you longing for God's strength and peace?

Today's Devotional

When God speaks, creation listens. His voice holds power, majesty, creativity, correction, and confidence, and it reshapes impossible circumstances. You can read Psalm 29 for a creative way to alter your thinking to consider God's perspective.

God the Father, and His Son, Jesus, could speak to creation and it would do exactly what They asked. Jesus calmed a storm for His disciples and God the Father turned back time for King Hezekiah. Jesus made a few fish and bread loaves into a meal for thousands and God the Father made an ax head float. Jesus healed a dead girl and God the Father helped the people of Israel win battles they had no reason to believe they could win.

The words God speaks are powerful. He spoke and this world came into existence. He spoke and mankind was offered rescue. He spoke and between every syllable He proved He loved you. He spoke and mercy received a summons.

The accumulation of these facts should leave you with comfort and infuse you with peace. This peace will make sense to a man who lives in a chaos that simply can't continue in the presence of God's voice.

Prayer

I need the peace that makes no sense to me, Lord. I need the help that only You can provide. I need You, and You want to help. Give me the wisdom to ask, seek, and knock rather than to search for creative but unwise alternatives.

Day 16
GOD OF GREATNESS

Read Psalm 48

Great is the LORD, and most worthy of praise,
in the city of our God, his holy mountain.
PSALM 48:1 NIV

Questions to Consider

- When was the last time you praised God for something more than what He's done for you? When have you praised Him purely for His extreme and supreme greatness?

- What person, place, or thing have you placed on a higher pedestal than God? When you set that entity next to God, how does it really compare?

- What thoughts fill your mind as you consider that God will be with you, guiding you forever?

Today's Devotional

If you're in the market for a car or a house, you'll want to do some comparison shopping. Big-ticket items demand extra time and attention, so we can be sure we're getting the best deal possible.

But you have to know what you're comparing. You

wouldn't compare a car with a house, for example. One is for transportation. One is for habitation. Because they have such different purposes, they don't lend themselves to a true comparison.

In a similar way, we must beware of comparing anything in this world to God. He is so far above and beyond His creation, that no person, place, thing, or idea can begin to reach Him. Nothing on this earth can be truly compared to the Lord. He is great and "most worthy of praise."

If anything, the disappointments we experience with people, places, things, and ideas should remind us of the awesome love, power, consistency, and goodness of our Lord. As the sons of Korah wrote in their conclusion to Psalm 48, "For this God is our God for ever and ever; he will be our guide even to the end" (verse 14 NIV).

Our God is a God of greatness. Don't let anything in this world interfere with His proper place in your heart.

Prayer

You are a great God. I can never go wrong with Your compassion, kindness, and awesomeness. May I never allow anything in this world to take Your place in my heart.

Day 17
GOD THE PROTECTOR

Read Psalm 91

There shall no evil befall thee, neither shall any plague
come nigh thy dwelling. For he shall give his angels
charge over thee, to keep thee in all thy ways.
Psalm 91:10–11 kjv

Questions to Consider

- Assuming that the promises of Psalm 91 depend on your meeting the conditions of its first two verses, how often do you dwell in "the secret place of the most High," abiding in God, acknowledging Him as your protector, and trusting Him for everything?

- What is God rescuing you from today? How does it feel knowing that no matter what comes against you, He's taking care of the details?

- Which of the promises in this psalm are speaking most to you today? Why?

Today's Devotional

Just try to imagine life apart from God's constant care. He knows everything that could happen to you, and many, many times, He intervenes. Some accidents never happen, because

God chose to head off a drunk driver. Some seemingly great but ultimately troublesome opportunities fall through because God knows better than you. He is in complete control.

God's protection might actually look like gridlock or missed opportunities. But His protection keeps you from avoidable pain.

Of course, God does allow us to experience trouble. But He also provides escape routes—at times and in ways we may never recognize. Sometimes we don't even consider thanking Him because we wrongly conclude that we were entirely on our own at the time.

Trust the God who does good things for you. Admit today that you are oblivious to much of His work in your life. The Lord begins with compassion, continues with kindness, and always finishes with His great love for you. He is your protector.

Prayer

*Thank You, Father, for protecting me from things
I never even considered. Thanks for keeping me
from worry that I don't need. Thanks for loving me
enough to do more for me than I ever knew.*

Day 18
GOD OF REFUGE

Read Psalm 94

Your unfailing love, O LORD, supported me. When doubts filled my mind, your comfort gave me renewed hope and cheer.
PSALM 94:18–19 NLT

Questions to Consider

- In what ways do God's words, ways, and promises provide relief for you in troubled times?

- When have you cried out to God because you thought you were falling or slipping only to discover He was supporting you? When doubts filled your mind, in what ways did God comfort you and infuse you with hope?

- How does it make you feel, knowing that in times of trouble, you have a place to go? How do you get to that place?

Today's Devotional

Your frame of reference helps determine what action you will take. If your frame of reference says you have to fight your battles alone, when enemies attack you'll find adrenaline coursing through your veins. However, if your frame of reference is to trust in God, there's a peace and ease that covers even unwanted situations. You know you are not—and never have been—alone.

God is your refuge, and you can depend on it. His love and comfort renew your hope and cheer, even in the heat of battle. Even in the dark of doubt.

We can all find relief in God as our refuge. He is a place to get out of the way of trouble. He will help us in our struggle.

You might think that seeking refuge isn't terribly manly. It's easy to believe the real goal is to stand and fight—all alone. But think about it: In the old west, men moved to a fort when threatened. Centuries before that, knights retreated behind the castle walls for refuge. Why do we think we need to do otherwise?

Going it alone rarely works. The good news is, God says you don't need to. *He* is always there for us.

Prayer

Lord, I commit myself to running to You. Don't let me confuse standing firm on my own with standing firm beside You. I need Your refuge. I need Your protection.

Day 19
GOD OF DELIVERANCE

Read Psalm 118

You are my God, and I will praise you; you are my God, and I will exalt you. Give thanks to the LORD, for he is good; his love endures forever.
PSALM 118:28–29 NIV

Questions to Consider

- God's mercy, love, and kindness never end. How are you changed knowing those things will follow you wherever you go?

- When was the last time you called on God while you lived the life of a struggler? How did His answer and deliverance help you?

- What would happen if you began each morning knowing that God is greater than anything you may face, rejoicing in the day He has made, and being intentional about your response?

Today's Devotional

Wrestle to hang on to the wisdom of retrospection. Look back and witness the footprints of a God who never left your side. Observe His handiwork. Praise the God who never leaves or abandons. Thank Him for His enduring love. This God is your great deliverer and His rescue can't be duplicated by anyone. His offer of rescue has always been yours for the asking.

There is no end to the good things God has waiting for you. Have you been dealing with irrational, negative people all day? God is a constant source of goodness. Have you encountered unfaithfulness from a friend or your spouse? Christ was faithful all the way to the cross as payment for your sins. Have you made a mistake and faced another person's wrath? God stands ready to offer forgiveness. Are you frightened? The Lord will never leave you nor forsake you. Do you feel unloved? The Father has loved you with an everlasting love.

It's okay to be a struggler. That puts you in a position to call on God for help. Then you can rejoice even before His help arrives, knowing God answers prayer.

Prayer

Lord God, sometimes Your greatest deliverance will be to rescue me from me. I can get in Your way, and I can get in my own way. Help me to accept Your perfect deliverance, for You are good.

Day 20
GOD OF PURPOSE

Read Isaiah 42:1–9

*Behold, the former things are come to pass, and new things
do I declare: before they spring forth I tell you of them.*
Isaiah 42:9 kjv

Questions to Consider

- How can God tell of "new things" before they even spring forth? How are topics such as creation, prophecy, and God's omniscience related?

- It is God who gives you breath as you stand upon the earth and spirit as you walk upon it. When do you recognize this the most?

- What new thing is God doing in your life?

Today's Devotional

Can you say who will win next year's Super Bowl? Oh, you might have an idea of which team has the best players and coaching staff. You might consider this year's results and try to project what might happen next season. But no human being can tell with absolute certainty what will happen in the next minute, let alone next year or a century from now.

But God can. Since He created time, He exists outside of

it. God is present in every moment, so He knows currently what is future to human beings. He can declare "new things," telling us all about them before they ever "spring forth."

That's how the prophet Micah could predict Bethlehem as the birthplace of Jesus. That's how Zechariah could picture the Lord's triumphal entry into Jerusalem with such precision. God has a plan and He has a view of everything that leads to that plan. And that's why we call Him the God of purpose.

Our world often seems random. Tornadoes and murders and diseases and explosions seem to "just happen," and people are affected in deep, difficult ways. While we can't fully explain God's purposes in all of these things, we know that He is aware of each and every one—and can work them together, in the lives of His children, "for good" (Romans 8:28).

Prayer

Lord, You are so far beyond me. Your purposes are sometimes mysterious, but I know that You have a good plan. Please give me faith to trust You.

Day 21
GOD OF FORGIVENESS

Read Isaiah 43:22–44:5

[God said] "I—yes, I alone—will blot out your sins for my own sake and will never think of them again."

ISAIAH 43:25 NLT

Questions to Consider

- What thoughts run through your mind as you consider that God forgives your sins, forgets your "miss takes," not because of your character but because of His own? That despite your sins, God continues to bless you in every way?

- What sins do you need to confess to God today—perhaps even sins you haven't yet admitted to yourself?

- How often do you praise God for His generous gift of forgiving and forgetting?

Today's Devotional

To be blunt, forgiveness means that wrong choices were made. Someone broke trust. It means that the one making wrong choices admits he was wrong. Forgiveness restores broken relationships. You can't forgive someone who has never offended you. That means that when you break God's law, He's the only one who can offer forgiveness.

Forgiveness is a gift you can receive *and* share. Let's talk about receiving His forgiveness for a minute. Are you holding on to a pet sin that you've been unwilling to give up? Let it go. Release it to the one who will never remember it or hold it against you. He will cast it far from you. Isn't that good news?

Now let's talk about extending forgiveness to others. In the same way that you make choices that offend God, others will undoubtedly make choices that offend you. You need God's forgiveness and others will need yours. Decide never to make the offender pay for his or her sins again. By holding on to a grudge, you are choosing to hold on to the pain it causes as you relive the offense over and over again. That's destructive behavior—and it's very unlike your God.

Prayer

You have forgiven me, and You have forgotten what I've done, Lord. Thank You. Help me to honor Your gift by forgiving others and restoring relationships that have been broken.

Day 22
GOD THE SERVANT

Read John 13:1–17

[Jesus] got up from the meal, took off his outer clothing, and wrapped a towel around his waist. After that, he poured water into a basin and began to wash his disciples' feet, drying them with the towel that was wrapped around him.

JOHN 13:4–5 NIV

Questions to Consider

- Jesus is God, the creator of the universe who became a servant and got down on His knees to wash the dirty, smelly feet of His disciples. When was the last time you did something as humbling? What were your thoughts at the time?

- How do you humbly yet happily serve others? What blessings have you experienced in doing so?

Today's Devotional

You go to a restaurant and tip for good service. You pay for a hotel room and expect that exceptional service comes standard. Some people will object to self-service lanes in stores because they believe personal service should be part of the shopping experience.

It's not hard to absorb the impact of what Jesus did in John 13. Jesus is the Son of God. He was with God the Father in the beginning. He lived in the presence of God before He came to earth. He performed miracles. If anyone deserved to be served, it was Jesus. Yet He did something no one expected—and some resisted. Jesus washed the feet of His disciples. This was dirty and unpleasant work. It was a bold visual statement to His followers.

Jesus didn't ask them to do something He would not do Himself. They saw firsthand that God's Son was a servant. It made a difference for the disciples. It's still making a difference through believers who serve the poor, the homeless, and the destitute in the name of Jesus.

Prayer

Lord Jesus, sometimes my human nature rebels against serving others. But You set the example of humble, loving service—not only by washing Your disciples' feet, but by dying on the cross for my sins. Help me to sacrifice my will for others, Lord. May I honor You by everything I do.

Day 23
GOD OF THE TRINITY

Read John 14

*"When the Father sends the Advocate as my representative—
that is, the Holy Spirit—he will teach you everything
and will remind you of everything I have told you."*
JOHN 14:26 NLT

Questions to Consider

- Jesus said that if you have seen Him, you have seen the Father. How does that change the way you think of God?

- Consider what Jesus said when He expressed that if you believe in Him, you will do even greater things than He did (John 14:12). He also said that whatever you ask, praying in His name, you'll receive. How do these promises offer peace?

- The Holy Spirit has many names, such as Comforter, Helper, and Spirit of Truth. By which name do you know Him best? Why?

Today's Devotional

Genesis 1:1 introduces God, who existed from eternity past and spoke the world into existence. John 1:1 introduces Jesus as someone who coexisted with God in the beginning.

John 14 talks about the Holy Spirit. These three are always One, referred to by Christians as the Trinity. There's never a best two out of three decision-making consultation between them. God the Father, Jesus the Son, and the Holy Spirit all work with the same truth, and toward the same goal. They are not three separate expressions of God; They are God.

Together, the Trinity creates, instructs, loves, and saves. Most Christians are familiar and comfortable with God the Father and Jesus the Son. But sometimes the Holy Spirit is overlooked. Perhaps that is because it's hard to visualize this Spirit. But His work is to teach and remind you of what God and Jesus have already said. The Spirit fills a believer's life, growing the spiritual fruit of love, joy, peace, and all the rest (Galatians 5:22–23).

The Holy Spirit is God living His life in and through you. It's truly an amazing thing.

Prayer

You do work that no one else can, Father. The unity You have with Jesus and the Holy Spirit means that Your rescue plan is fully realized. As a Christian, I can learn more about You with Your Spirit as my instructor.

Day 24
GOD THE LIFE-GIVER

Read John 15:1–16:16

[Jesus said], "I am the vine; you are the branches. If you remain in me and I in you, you will bear much fruit; apart from me you can do nothing."
JOHN 15:5 NIV

Questions to Consider

- Jesus says that to bear fruit, you must abide (or dwell) in Him, for without Him, you can do nothing. How has this been tested and proven in your own life?

- What thoughts come to mind when you consider that you did not choose Jesus, but He chose you to bear fruit and receive whatever you ask for in prayer?

- Reflect on the fact that Jesus loves you and has sent the Holy Spirit to guide you. In what ways does this give you life?

Today's Devotional

Sweet, juicy grapes—designed by God to bring nourishment and pleasure into human lives. Jesus used the imagery of the grapevine to teach us some very important truths.

The Lord identified Himself as "the vine," the main

support for all of His followers, "the branches." When we stay connected to Him, getting our live-giving sustenance from His infinite, healthy supply, we produce "fruit"—which the apostle Paul later defined as "love, joy, peace, patience, kindness, goodness, faithfulness, gentleness, and self-control" (Galatians 5:22–23 NLT).

But when a branch is separated from the vine, it stops producing fruit. It doesn't even have life anymore. The branch quickly dries out and becomes useless. Branches off a vine are hardly even worth tossing onto a fire.

When you're actively and consciously with God, though, part of His family by faith in Jesus Christ, you will grow. You'll lengthen and strengthen and produce a sweet fruit that others can enjoy. Your love, joy, and peace—and every Christian virtue—will bring nourishment and pleasure to those around you. You'll share with others the life that God has given you.

Sound good? Just "remain" in Jesus.

Prayer

When I do things on my own, Lord, I become less than I should be. I wither and wilt. Keep me securely attached to Your vine so I can produce life-giving fruit.

Day 25
GOD THE SAVIOR

Read John 19:1–37

*[Jesus] bearing his cross went forth into a place
called the place of a skull, which is called in the
Hebrew Golgotha: Where they crucified him.*
JOHN 19:17–18 KJV

Questions to Consider

- How might this story have turned out differently if the
  people who played a role in executing Jesus had actually
  known Him as God the Savior?

- Is reading this account difficult emotionally and spiritually? Why or why not?

- Which person in this story do you find it hardest to
  identify with? The easiest to identify with? Besides Jesus,
  of whom are you the most proud? Of whom are you the
  most ashamed? What qualities might you share with each
  of these characters?

Today's Devotional

History is filled with events that were condemned in hindsight but seemed like a perfect response at the moment. The
crucifixion of Jesus was one of those events. It was a choice

sanctioned by religious leaders, championed by popular opinion, and accepted by political leaders who thought it best not to wage a war for one man—even though the politicians saw nothing wrong in Him.

Emotions can get the best of our collective response. Peer pressure can influence events to move in a less-than-ideal direction. But this scenario, when applied to Jesus, proves that God can take bad circumstances and turn them into exceptional outcomes. All the horrific things that happened to Jesus led to something that was essential to completing the requirements needed for Him to become the Savior of the world and provide a rescue plan that would be available to all.

No one is outside God's ability to rescue. Not you or the person who's made life hard for you. Because relationships mean so much to God, He made it possible for you to come back to Him and then stay close. And, hopefully, bring many others with you.

Prayer

Father God, You can take a bad circumstance and make it good through the life of Your Son, Jesus. Help me remember that You do the same for me.

Day 26
GOD OF THE RESURRECTION

Read Mark 16

The angel said, "Don't be alarmed. You are looking for Jesus of Nazareth, who was crucified. He isn't here! He is risen from the dead! Look, this is where they laid his body."

MARK 16:6 NLT

Questions to Consider

- The female followers of Jesus were the first to arrive at His tomb, ready to go about the normal duties following the death of a loved one, and were shocked to find the stone covering of the tomb rolled away. When were you last surprised by the God of the resurrection? What did you learn from the experience?

- When did you first believe in the resurrected God? How is He working in your life today?

Today's Devotional

Though He was truly a king, Jesus didn't come across that way. He wasn't born where most people expected. He didn't live with a family that others considered royal. He didn't have the customary upbringing of someone with authority. He also didn't lie, cheat, steal, or otherwise take advantage of people.

Many people hated Him. Some liked Him. A few loved Him above all other things. As they watched Him die, the world seemed smaller. A few of His most passionate followers went to His tomb at the accustomed time for preparing deceased bodies. That is, after all, what they expected to find.

They had heard what Jesus said about "rising" in three days. As with His parables, with meanings veiled from many listeners, those words might be just another thing people couldn't understand. Sure, a handful of people had risen from the dead by the command of a living Jesus. But how could He bring Himself back to life?

And yet He did. When Jesus arose, all of His disciples struggled to comprehend what they assumed was impossible. At some time or another, we've all had the same response. And we've all been given the same message: "Don't be alarmed! He is risen from the dead!"

Prayer

Lord God, You proved that Your power was stronger than death. You proved that Your love can lead to eternal life. You proved You weren't just part of history but rather, the maker of history.

Day 27
GOD OUR FRIEND

Read 1 John 1:1–2:14

*If we claim to be without sin, we deceive ourselves
and the truth is not in us. If we confess our sins,
he is faithful and just and will forgive us our
sins and purify us from all unrighteousness.*
1 JOHN 1:8–9 NIV

Questions to Consider

- God cared for you so much that He came to earth to show you the way back to Him. You can now be a friend to God like Adam and his fellow creation Eve before the fall.

- How does knowing God loves you this much help you to love and befriend others?

- In what ways can you make sure the light of God reflects through you, to others, during life's dark moments?

Today's Devotional

Jesus died for friendship. He endured the cross to rescue His friends. He defeated death to give His friends meaning beyond death. Jesus has proven beyond a shadow of a doubt that He is more than worthy to bear the title of friend.

You can lie to yourself but God knows better. If you could

keep His law 100 percent of the time, the death of Jesus was meaningless. But you can't obey like that. So God invites His friends to do something other than pretending to be perfect. He invites you to confess the ways you've broken His law. He calls you admit that He was right and you were wrong. This isn't to force you to say things you don't want to say. It's just that God wants you to understand and believe the truth of His divine rescue—you cannot save yourself.

The result of your confession is a life that acts like a mirror. You begin to reflect who God really is so others can see Him too. They'll want to know the Friend who has so dramatically changed your life.

Prayer

I am weak, and You are strong, Lord. You take friendship seriously and will help when I ask. Thank You for being the very best of friends. Keep me from the sinful urge to hide from You.

Day 28
GOD THE PRAISEWORTHY

Read Revelation 4:1–5:14

*Thou art worthy, O Lord, to receive glory and
honour and power: for thou hast created all things,
and for thy pleasure they are and were created.*
REVELATION 4:11 KJV

Questions to Consider

- Have you ever "seen" God on His throne in the heavenlies?
  If not, how could you focus your spiritual eyes on that
  scene? How did you (or would you) respond?

- What three aspects of God do you consider most
  praiseworthy?

- Imagine your prayers in the golden bowls of incense held
  by heavenly creatures as they sing songs of praise to Jesus.
  How might that imagery change the way you pray?

Today's Devotional

People who spend time with God will discover an attitude of
praise that changes the way they think, act, and respond. It's
difficult to stand in the presence of God and leave unchanged.

God is continuously worthy, but you must assign a value
to being with Him. Does it help you or not? Do you find

renewed hope or despair? Do you experience His love more personally? Once you assign worth to your meeting with God you begin to see that all creation exists to honor Him. You can't witness things like the Grand Canyon, Victoria Falls, or the Great Barrier Reef and not consider the handiwork and creativity of God.

Take some time and think about what God has done for you. Once you have a list, take some more time to thank Him for each thing—and remember the experience of living within His good pleasure.

God can and will do what only He's capable of. Witness, be astounded, and honor Him with praise.

Prayer

You do what I cannot, God. My life is enhanced because of Your work that I could never do on my own. I want to recognize Your goodness and respond with words and actions that demonstrate how worthy You are.

Day 29
GOD OF SALVATION

Read Revelation 19

*After this, I heard what sounded like a vast crowd
in heaven shouting, "Praise the LORD! Salvation
and glory and power belong to our God."*
REVELATION 19:1 NLT

Questions to Consider

- Within the first four verses of this reading, three times various heavenly creatures shout "Praise the LORD!" for God's salvation, glory, and power. How often do you think or say those words? How could you use them more often?

- Imagine heaven opening, revealing a white horse whose rider is called Faithful and True. Jesus, the Son of God, is coming to defeat all evil, to save your very life. What would you say to the God of your salvation?

Today's Devotional

People accept the truth of Jesus when the light of His salvation dawns and a whole new world opens to a heart that welcomes His life-altering work. One by one men and women join a chorus of voices that are entirely comfortable whispering, singing, or shouting the words recorded in Revelation

19:1—"Praise the LORD! Salvation and glory and power belong to our God."

It's true that some people cannot honestly project their voice in Jesus' favor. For unbelievers, those not born again, praise would be inauthentic and hypocritical. On the other hand, it's wrong for people who have accepted Jesus' salvation to keep silent.

Take a moment to think about what you've been saved from. Consider the road you were on, and see if that destination was better than where believers in Jesus are headed. Your salvation improves your life on earth and guarantees you eternal life with the God who made you, keeps you, and always plans for your best.

Having accepted and enjoyed that salvation, be sure to make an invitation to others.

Prayer

Lord God, Your grace through Jesus is enough.
His gift is eternal. His love is changing me.
Let me not be silent about such a great gift.

Day 30
GOD THE APPROACHABLE

Read Revelation 22

They will see his face, and his name will be on their foreheads. There will be no more night. They will not need the light of a lamp or the light of the sun, for the Lord God will give them light. And they will reign for ever and ever.
REVELATION 22:4–5 NIV

Questions to Consider

- Someday you will find yourself dwelling eternally with God in a beautiful place, having a relationship with Him like Adam had before the fall. What would be the first thing you'll say or do when you see God personally?

- In what ways do you acknowledge God's presence in your everyday activities? How do you approach Him?

- As you have gotten to know God better, how much more do you sense that He is showing up in your life? What's the most important thing He wants you to know?

Today's Devotional

God is not as unapproachable as some believe Him to be. You don't have to book an appointment and wait to speak to Him. He is a 24/7 God. He never sleeps. He is always available to listen as you approach Him in prayer. And because He is infinite, God can and will listen to everyone who calls on Him—you'll never get His voice mail.

God's Word suggests you can (and should) come to Him in boldness, and this line of communication can remain open for the rest of your life. It is more appropriate to admit that you have needs than to hide the fact, even if your intentions seem good.

If it were possible for your soul to breathe a sigh of relief, then this would be the right time and a perfect reason to relax—knowing that your concerns, questions, and confessions are what God is seeking from you. He already knows everything. But He likes to hear your own personal assessment of your needs. Be honest with God. Approach Him with your cares, because He certainly cares for you.

Prayer

*May the words I speak to You reflect what is
truly happening in the deepest parts of me, Lord.
Thanks for inviting me to share everything.*

30 DAYS OF BIBLE READINGS FOR KNOWING JESUS BETTER

*I want to know Christ—yes, to know
the power of his resurrection.*
PHILIPPIANS 3:10 NIV

A camera can focus on only one small slice of life. But put many photos into an album or slideshow, and you begin to get a fuller, more satisfying view.

Over the next thirty days you'll be reading about Jesus. His love permeates the Bible, and you will either enjoy your first exposure or become reacquainted with the Savior of humanity. His mission to earth was wrapped tightly in the power of love.

Each day you'll experience a snapshot of Jesus' life—a single slice of His love and an image of the new life He has for you. Over thirty days, let this panoramic display of Jesus' life transform you. It becomes both a quest and a destination.

Before you read each scripture passage, pray. Ask for wisdom to understand what you read. Believe that God has something to tell you, then seek until you find Him. You will learn to know God's voice as He describes Jesus through His Word.

Follow your reading with meditation—a time when you explore what you're learning. Take notes and revisit the quest at the end of this month. Your goal is simple: knowing Jesus better. What could possibly be more important?

Day 1
THE BIRTH OF JESUS [PART 1]

Read Matthew 1:18–25

This is how the birth of Jesus the Messiah came
about: His mother Mary was pledged to be married
to Joseph, but before they came together, she was
found to be pregnant through the Holy Spirit.
MATTHEW 1:18 NIV

Questions to Consider

- When has God stepped into your dreams and given you a new direction to follow? Did you follow His redirection or stubbornly stick to your already well-laid-out path?

- Have you obeyed God in a situation when He asked you to do what seemed to go against tradition, public opinion, and societal norms? What happened?

- How have your expectations and God's plans differed? How do you allow room for God to speak into your life, separating your inner conversation from His divine voice?

Today's Devotional

What would you do if it seemed that God was asking you to do something unusual or that His plan for you included elements that defied logic? It could mean leaving a well-paying job or introducing Jesus to someone who has never had anything but hatred for God. It feels safer and easier to dismiss these divine prompts in favor of the status quo.

Mary had one of those moments. She planned to marry a local carpenter and quietly raise a family. It certainly held elements of contentment and normalcy. But Mary's plan was not God's plan. She would bear God's Son even though she had never yet been with a man. To the curious it would seem Mary had either been unfaithful to Joseph or that they hadn't waited for marriage. Neither was true, but there are always those who will assume. . .and talk.

God chose the unconventional. He was demonstrating that He has the power to defy conventional wisdom. His way of doing things won't always match the way human beings would. In fact, they often don't. But His way is always better.

Prayer

Lord, please help me remember that what You ask me to do only needs to make sense to You. Give me the courage to follow when You say, "Let's go!"

Day 2
THE BIRTH OF JESUS [PART 2]

Read Luke 2:1–20

[Mary] brought forth her firstborn son, and wrapped him in swaddling clothes, and laid him in a manger; because there was no room for them in the inn.
LUKE 2:7 KJV

Questions to Consider

- When have you discovered God's glory amidst challenging and unfair circumstances? How did you respond?

- What unexpected happenings in your life have prompted you to ponder God's amazing orchestration of human events?

- Does it change your perspective to realize that God often uses ordinary, even lowly, people to carry His message and bring change to the world?

Today's Devotional

In today's reading, Mary and Joseph reaffirmed their commitment to each other—and to God. A less-than-voluntary journey brought the couple to Bethlehem for a Roman census. In this "city of David," the king who was an ancestor of both of them, Mary and Joseph discovered there was no room in an inn. As Mary began labor with God's Son they found lodging space with farm animals. This was where the most important human being who ever lived drew His first breath. Challenging? Yes. Unfair? Perhaps. God's plan? Absolutely.

The first people told to seek out Jesus and worship Him were shepherds. These men were social outcasts. People often found offense with them, perhaps in part because shepherds generally smelled like the animals they cared for. Perhaps this was God's way of symbolizing that He, too, cared for "sheep"—wayward people—in a way many wouldn't understand. But it was certainly the type of care they needed.

Jesus' adventure was a surprise to everyone. But with the benefit of hindsight we can see why He refused to demand any special privileges. He was entitled to every comfort and honor this world could have provided. But by His humble birth, Jesus proved He really had come for all.

Prayer

Heavenly Father, Your Son did not arrive into exclusive circumstances. He humbled Himself more than anyone ever had, and in doing so became relatable to all mankind. Thank You for being so inclusive.

Day 3
THE WISE MEN'S VISIT

Read Matthew 2:1–12

*[The wise men] entered the house and saw the child
with his mother, Mary, and they bowed down and
worshiped him. Then they opened their treasure chests
and gave him gifts of gold, frankincense, and myrrh.*
MATTHEW 2:11 NLT

Questions to Consider

- How far do you feel you've had to travel to find and worship Jesus, the King? What did your search reveal?

- When was the last time you gave Jesus a gift? What was its significance to you? How do you think it was received?

- Has God ever warned you about something, through a dream or another person's words or some other method? Can you allow God's counsel to override conventional wisdom?

Today's Devotional

The wise men probably didn't arrived in Bethlehem the night Jesus was born. It took a while to follow the star. These "magi" would have had arrangements to make prior to leaving home. There was likely no competition between the shepherds and the wise men around the Lord's manger.

The wise men (no number of these travelers is mentioned in scripture) recognized that Jesus was worth an immense journey. Their long and tiring trip would end in a time of worship and the giving of gifts that spoke of Jesus' royalty—and their choice to honor Him.

Yesterday you read of the arrival of shepherds, among the least honored men in Jewish society. Today you read of men, who might have been kings themselves, who arrived to honor God's Son. This feels like a strong indication that Jesus fit with the rich as well as the poor. It seems He came to reach those with little influence, as well as those with much. Whatever your social status, God sent Jesus for you.

Prayer

You know who I am, Lord. You sent Your Son
for me—knowing my exact status and struggles.
Thanks for making that clear in Your Word.

Day 4
THE WORD BECAME FLESH

Read John 1:1–28

*In the beginning was the Word, and the Word was with God,
and the Word was God. He was with God in the beginning.*
JOHN 1:1–2 NIV

Questions to Consider

- What does it mean to you that Jesus is *the* Word who speaks all things into being and sustains all things— including you? What is Jesus speaking and sustaining in your life today?

- What comes to mind when you realize that—because you believe in Jesus—you are God's son, with all the birthrights and privileges that go with that?

- Have you ever felt like John the Baptist, a lone voice crying in the wilderness? Why or why not?

Today's Devotional

Jesus would have known the location of the tree that would one day be used to crucify Him. He knew all about the ore which would someday comprise the spikes used to hold Him to the tree. He created the dirt that would be removed from the hole where His cross would be planted. He knew the men who would beat Him, the people who would mock Him, and the hearts of the disciples who would run away when He was arrested. He knew all of this long before He stepped forward as the Savior. He knew these things eternally before He became a flesh-and-blood human.

The arrival of Jesus was heralded by John the Baptist. It was welcomed by many who saw Him as the Jews' rescuer from Rome's oppression. Many people misunderstood why Jesus came. They could not believe that this man of such spiritual influence was destined for the death of a common criminal.

But that was all part of God's plan. Jesus is God's Word, spoken and declared to the hearts of humankind. He is the new agreement, the new covenant between God and man, the only way we can be reconciled. Jesus is the possibility of a God who won't accept the impossible. He is the Word by which we grasp hope—both now and forever.

Prayer

May the words of my mouth accept the Word You
sent to live here, Father. Jesus is the Word You
want me to accept. Help me hear His voice.

Day 5
A LIGHT HAS RISEN

Read Matthew 4:12–17

*"The people who sat in darkness have seen a great
light. And for those who lived in the land where
death casts its shadow, a light has shined."*
MATTHEW 4:16 NLT

Questions to Consider

- Have you felt as if you were being swallowed by darkness?
What did you think and feel? How did you get back into
God's light?

- Where do you go when you are discouraged, when you (or
people you love) are imprisoned spiritually, emotionally,
or physically? Why does that place soothe you?

- What are some Bible verses that keep you from being
overcome by darkness? How does the Word keep you in
the light?

Today's Devotional

Think of light as possibility, perspective, and hope. Life
circumstances often place you in a dark corner where your
imagination enlarges the negatives and ignores the positives.
It is a place of desperation. It promotes fear and distrust.

This darkness is the birthplace of loneliness, a home where lawbreaking finds a welcome.

When light comes, the filth and decay are exposed. But the light also illuminates a path that leads away from the grime. It reveals what's been hidden. While that may feel bad at first, it's not. Light allows you to see your missteps, so you can see the next positive steps to take. Darkness apart from God is infinitely worse than a darkness dispelled by His light. He shows you His path, then leads you along that path.

Light corrects faulty conclusions, reveals the lies you believed in the darkness, and enhances your ability to understand the world around you.

Jesus came to earth to bring that light. He brought hope to a world settling for apathy. He brought clarity to a world wallowing in spiritual confusion. His light is still shining in dark places. If you need light, ask Him for it.

Prayer

Thank You for the light that helps me see things the way they really are, Lord. I can witness the good, the bad, and the awful—and that allows me to make better decisions.

Day 6
JESUS' MINISTRY IN GALILEE

Read Luke 4:14–37

*Then [Jesus] rolled up the scroll, gave it back to
the attendant and sat down. The eyes of everyone
in the synagogue were fastened on him.*
LUKE 4:20 NIV

Questions to Consider

- Is it your custom, as it was Jesus' (see Luke 4:16), to attend church every week? Why or why not?

- Have you ever gone "home" and been poorly treated by people because of your faith? How could you "walk through the crowd" and go on your way?

- In which situations has Jesus come and healed your broken heart? Liberated your imprisoned spirit? Given your mind new insight? Set your soul free from oppression?

Today's Devotional

Jesus brought something unique to anyone who would listen to His words. But there were those who dismissed His position as God's Son because He lacked a title, prestige, or an impressive occupation. People faulted Jesus for His home address. They made faulty conclusions their go-to response.

The people Jesus grew up with did not treat Him well. It seemed a sizable portion of the population said in their words and actions, "You don't impress me much."

They were looking for the accolades, the certification, the better family. Jesus just didn't measure up in their eyes. Sure, He was unique and interesting, but they considered this to be a dangerous thing.

Jesus came to His own and they didn't receive Him. At least not at first. Even His own family tried to convince Him to tone things down. Most in His hometown continued to overlook the fact that He was God's Son.

But there were some who chose to listen. There were those who paid no attention to Jesus' resume. He spoke truth, and some people recognized it. He offered life, and some accepted it. He came on a rescue mission, and many were rescued.

Prayer

I am nothing without You, Lord, and I have no reason to judge Your perfection. I choose to accept You for who You are and what You've done for me.

Day 7
JESUS' TRUE FAMILY

Read Mark 3:13–35

*Whosoever shall do the will of God, the same
is my brother, and my sister, and mother.*
MARK 3:35 KJV

Questions to Consider

- Jesus calls to Himself those with whom He wants to work. When did Jesus call you? How has your life changed as a result?

- What task has Jesus called you to pursue with Him? How do you tap into His power to do what He asks?

- Those men who do God's will are Jesus' brothers. How does it feel to claim that privilege? How might your attitudes change if you kept your role as "brother of Jesus" uppermost in your thoughts?

Today's Devotional

Does Mark 3:35 sound harsh and ungrateful? If it does, then it probably requires some extra thought. Reread today's entire passage and ask the Lord for insight. What might God be trying to teach you through these verses?

Is it possible that Jesus is dismissing His family as not

important? If this is true, would He be showing the honor God said we should have for parents? What if Jesus was simply pointing out that while we have an earthly family we also have a spiritual family, and this family does not depend on things as trivial as where you were born, what street you live on, the color of your skin, or how much you earn?

Those who accept God, join His quest, and follow Him are family members in a spiritual sense. They learn to depend on each other, enjoy mutual encouragement, and walk with other family members. As a Christian you are counted as a brother to Jesus. You are adopted into His family. And this process begins with believing and accepting Him. An enhanced family dynamic will follow.

Prayer

Lord God, You are my Father, and I am a son. I am loved, adopted, and welcomed into Your family as the brother of Jesus! There are many others, and they are my family too. Help me to treat them that way.

Day 8
JESUS CLEANSES THE TEMPLE AND MEETS WITH NICODEMUS

Read John 2:12–3:21

There was a man named Nicodemus, a Jewish
religious leader who was a Pharisee. After dark
one evening, he came to speak with Jesus.
JOHN 3:1–2 NLT

Questions to Consider

- Have you ever given material things and mental "transactions" priority over prayer and worship of God? How so?

- What do you think when you realize that Jesus knows exactly what you're thinking?

- What changes occurred in your life after your spirit was born of God's Spirit? How do you nourish the "new you"?

Today's Devotional

Some say it is easier for children to accept the truth of Jesus than it is for adults. Children are less prone to be cynical. Adults find it harder to accept things that don't already fit their preconceived belief systems. The claims of a man who lived two thousand years ago can be extremely difficult to consider seriously.

But even in His day, Jesus seemed to cause the Jewish religious leaders more than a little heartburn. He talked about God as personal and loving. The scribes and Pharisees thought of God as impersonal, aloof, and only really for a select few. Jesus surrounded Himself with common men who had common jobs, and none had the credentials the religious leaders thought were important. As a "nobody," Jesus kept advancing His cause in unconventional ways.

Nicodemus, though, was a religious leader who had seen enough of Jesus to wonder if there was more than met the eye. Curious, Nicodemus went to Jesus, alone and after dark, so he could learn more. By the time he left, this man's faulty spiritual foundation was cracked and in need of repair. But of course Jesus was happy to help out. "You must be born again," He said (John 3:7 NLT).

Prayer

Keep me from being a know-it-all, God. Make me pliable. Destroy my old way of thinking and teach me Your ways.

Day 9
PARABLES OF JESUS

Read Mark 4:1–34

*[Jesus told His disciples], "The secret of the kingdom
of God has been given to you. But to those on
the outside everything is said in parables."*
MARK 4:11 NIV

Questions to Consider

- Which of the parables in Mark 11 speaks most clearly to your soul? Why?

- How have you prepared the "ground" of your heart to accept the seed of God's Word? What "fruit" is your life producing?

- Have you considered that time spent reading and studying God's Word results in greater wisdom? When have you seen that happen in your life?

Today's Devotional

Parables are stories that have two meanings. When Jesus told parables some may have thought He was offering instructions on agricultural practices or house cleaning. Others probably concluded that Jesus meant more than the story seemed to suggest. Even His disciples had to be told what spiritual truth was connected to the stories they heard. Jesus told the disciples He was giving them "the secret of the kingdom of God."

With the benefit of the whole Bible and plenty of teaching, most Christians today generally understand the meaning of Jesus' parables. But if you've discussed those little stories with unbelievers, you know that many people think of the parables as strange, even as gibberish. Satan has blinded people's spiritual eyes, keeping them from true understanding.

You could say that parables are a type of coded language for believers. But don't ever think you have any part of scripture down pat. God's Word, being "alive and active" (Hebrews 4:12 NIV), is always ready to take you further into His heart. Jesus' parables, simple as they may seem, will never be exhausted on this side of heaven.

Prayer

Your Word is filled with stories, Lord. I can read about Abraham, Noah, and Paul, and I can read the stories Jesus shared with His followers. As I read and study them, enlighten my mind with Your truth.

Day 10
THE HEART OF HUMANKIND

Read Mark 7

*Then Jesus called to the crowd to come and hear.
"All of you listen," he said, "and try to understand.
It's not what goes into your body that defiles you;
you are defiled by what comes from your heart."*

MARK 7:14–15 NLT

Questions to Consider

- Have you ever found yourself praising Jesus with your lips while your heart was somewhere else? How can you better align your heart with Jesus' heart?

- What have you been persistently praying about recently? How might God be using this experience in prayer to test your faith?

- What is Jesus laying on your heart today?

Today's Devotional

Jeremiah 17:9 (NLT) says, "The human heart is the most deceitful of all things, and desperately wicked. Who really knows how bad it is?"

Well, God does. He always has.

When you want to know more about Jesus, know this:

He's not someone who will tell you to search your heart for good answers. Jesus actually said you get spiritually filthy by what you discover in your heart. You can't keep it clean, and it will lie to you constantly. This may be why your heart is where God chooses to live, by your faith in Jesus and the sending of His Holy Spirit. If God is going to have an effect on your heart He will need to clean it up, personally and from the inside.

The Bible never encourages you to believe in yourself. You're supposed to believe in God! And scripture doesn't ask you to trust your instincts but rather God's truth. Your heart isn't fit for human habitation—but you can turn the keys over to the best resident it's ever had: Jesus.

Prayer

Lord, Your view of the heart is very different than most people's. I want to trust You rather than my own deceitful heart. Please change me from the inside out.

Day 11
EQUALITY WITH GOD

Read John 5

[Jesus said], "Very truly I tell you, the Son can do nothing by himself; he can do only what he sees his Father doing, because whatever the Father does the Son also does. For the Father loves the Son and shows him all he does. Yes, and he will show him even greater works than these."

JOHN 5:19–20 NIV

Questions to Consider

- Why might John have recorded the strange story of an angel stirring the waters of Bethesda for people's healing? How does the description of that kind of healing contrast with the healings Jesus performed?

- Which more closely describes you: a follower of rules or a follower of the Rule Maker? How do the two titles compare?

- Have you "searched the scriptures" to find eternal life? How do the scriptures "testify" about Jesus?

Today's Devotional

Philippians 2:6 (NIV) says that Jesus, "being in very nature God, did not consider equality with God something to be used to his own advantage." This verse says two key things. The first is that Jesus is equal with God—not greater or lesser. The second is that while He lived among us He did not use His supreme power to make life easier for Himself. His goal was to do what God wanted Him to accomplish.

Jesus would have been within His rights to skip the crucifixion, as well as the mockery and beatings that preceded it. He could have vanished when moments of confrontation arose. But He chose to live like one of us—and that meant without some of the benefits of being God.

Jesus chose to do what God the Father asked. His actions were a reflection of God's heart. His choices were in harmony with God's directive. His rescue of humankind was the fulfillment of a plan that had long been in the works.

Prayer

It is so easy to "claim my rights," God. I don't want to be inconvenienced by the actions of others and yet that is exactly what Jesus did. Thank You for being so compassionate.

Day 12
SERMON ON THE MOUNT [PART 1]

Read Matthew 5

Let your light so shine before men, that they may see your good works, and glorify your Father which is in heaven.
MATTHEW 5:16 KJV

Questions to Consider

- Which of the "blessed are" statements (see Matthew 5:3–10) seem to apply to you? How do they provide comfort or strength?

- In what ways are you letting your light shine so that your good works can point others to God?

- Who is Jesus prompting you to forgive today? Which enemy is He prompting you to bless?

- How might your following Jesus' instructions every day become a habit?

Today's Devotional

It's not as though everything Jesus taught defied conventional logic, but He did point to areas in which men's logic failed them. For instance most men believe things like "revenge is sweet," "pull yourself up by your own bootstraps," and "do whatever you have to in order to be successful."

The Sermon on the Mount challenged many notions that were largely accepted then and equally accepted now. Matthew 5 suggests that the poor in spirit receive the kingdom of God, those who mourn are comforted, strength under control leads to God's inheritance, those who long after God get God, those who show mercy receive mercy, the pure experience God, and the peacemakers look and act like God's children.

There's more in the passage, but this sample suggests that you can learn a lot from a God who is defined by justice rather than pettiness. He hates sin but loves those who sometimes choose to sin. He is also defined by mercy, which is His preferred gift.

Jesus' Sermon on the Mount provides course corrections for every day. In His love for us, God chose to show us the way we should go.

Prayer

Lord, we human beings can make wild assumptions about You and the life You've given us. Help me to seek Your Word to discover the way You want me to go and grow.

Day 13
SERMON ON THE MOUNT (PART 2)

Read Matthew 6

*"[God] your Father knows exactly what
you need even before you ask him!"*
MATTHEW 6:8 NLT

Questions to Consider

- Where is your secret place of prayer? What is it like? How often do you go there?

- How does seeking God's kingdom first help you to forgive others, lay up treasures in heaven, keep you loyal to God instead of money, and stave off worrying about tomorrow?

- What behind-the-scenes kindness can you perform for someone, a deed that's just between you and God? When you do, observe what reward you receive from God as a result.

Today's Devotional

Let's run through another batch of beliefs that gain perspective through the teachings of Jesus. 1) A kindness on your part can be private with no expectation of public applause. 2) Pray privately to an audience of one. 3) Your prayers can be personal and well thought through before you call on God.

4) Forgive others if you believe it's important to be forgiven by God. 5) When you fast no one needs to know about it. 6) Earth is a terrible place to hide treasure. However, heaven is perfect for this purpose. 7) Serve God alone—never money. 8) Always choose trusting God over worrying about anything.

How do these ideas conflict with the way you typically manage these issues? Do you expect or desire people to notice when you do the right thing? Are you disappointed when they don't? Is anything more important to you than a friendship with God? Is worry a closer friend than God?

As Jesus preached the Sermon on the Mount His hearers had plenty of things to consider. Those things were written down so *you* could consider them too. Today is a perfect day to do that.

Prayer

Lord, sometimes it's hard to accept that You are the only one who needs to know when I do good. Please tame my pride and help me be content in Your "well done."

Day 14
SERMON ON THE MOUNT [PART 3]

Read Matthew 7

When Jesus had finished saying these things, the crowds were amazed at his teaching, because he taught as one who had authority, and not as their teachers of the law.
MATTHEW 7:28–29 NIV

Questions to Consider

- What would your thoughts and words be like if you chose not to judge others? If you avoid judgment, how does that draw others closer to God?

- How would your life change if you treated everyone—regardless of who they are or what they have done—just as *you* would want to be treated?

- How persistent are you in asking, seeking, and knocking? Why would God demand such hard work in making requests of Him?

Today's Devotional

The Sermon on the Mount began with a series of unexpected blessings, continued with challenging thoughts, and moved on to inspired instruction. When it ended, people were amazed. They realized that they had heard something with the ability to change their lives.

Jesus' words included six more instructions that challenged the perspective of each guest. 1) Judging, while not forbidden, carries with it some stringent terms. 2) God can be approached, so ask, seek, and knock in prayer. 3) Follow God in the way He chooses and not in ways that seem more convenient. 4) Some who say they speak for God don't. 5) Some who say they follow God don't. 6) Wise men choose to obey and follow while foolish men don't and face destruction.

Jesus' message was a revelation. He spoke this truth so that discerning listeners (and readers) would understand: apart from God nothing is as it seems.

Prayer

Lord God, help me to understand that when You say You are in control, You really are in control. You don't need my help, though You welcome my involvement. You don't need my thoughts, though You listen to me. May I always recognize Your supremacy.

Day 15
POWER OVER THE PHYSICAL WORLD

Read Luke 8:22–56

*[The disciples] came to him, and awoke him,
saying, Master, master, we perish. Then he arose,
and rebuked the wind and the raging of the water:
and they ceased, and there was a calm.*

LUKE 8:24 KJV

Questions to Consider

- What does it mean to you that Jesus could actually calm a physical storm? Why can you believe that Jesus is always "in the boat" with you?

- When have you felt the power of Jesus diminishing the trouble in your life? Has Jesus ever turned your fear into wonder?

- What power do the words "be not afraid, only believe" hold for you? How would life change if you lived by these words?

Today's Devotional

You will remember that the Bible makes clear that Jesus set aside His rights as God to live the life of a human being. The way God healed people and calmed a storm exhibited

His power. He didn't do these things to help Himself or be more comfortable. On the Sea of Galilee, Jesus was awakened by His terrified disciples, crying out for their lives. For their benefit Jesus told the storm to cease. Then He expressed sorrow that the disciples set faith aside in favor of fear.

Jesus' power over the world He created was not something new or unique. He regularly told sickness to take a hike. He told evil spirits they were no longer welcome. He even restored life to people who had died. And Jesus told His disciples that *they* had the power to move mountains, by their faith in Him. In every instance, Jesus' power was used for the benefit of others.

This is a potent reminder that when Jesus steps into your worst-case scenario He has complete control. Your fears, however big they seem, are nothing in comparison to your Lord.

Prayer

Thank You, Lord, for showing me that You are firmly in control of everything that brings fear to my doorstep. Help me to trust You fully.

Day 16
POWER TO HEAL (PART 1)

Read Matthew 8:1–17

*Jesus said to the Roman officer, "Go back home.
Because you believed, it has happened." And the
young servant was healed that same hour.*
MATTHEW 8:13 NLT

Questions to Consider

- When asking Jesus for healing, how are you like or unlike this Roman soldier who expressed his personal unworthiness, then declared his faith by saying he knew Jesus *could* heal his servant?

- Neither time nor distance can impede Jesus' healing power. What does that tell you about Jesus' power in your life?

- What does it mean that Jesus doesn't simply heal but actually takes all illnesses and injuries on Himself?

Today's Devotional

You might think that modern medicine is a miracle, but when Jesus visited humankind His word was enough. He could proclaim healing and the one in search of healing went home whole. The cure was instantaneous. And the healed person didn't have to come back for a checkup.

In Matthew 8 you read of more than one healing. The passage starts with a man suffering from a contagious skin condition and ends with a believing Gentile soldier. No one *deserves* this kind of personal service from God, and the truth is that not everyone who wants healing receives it. You can pray for a cure, but God may have His own reasons for saying no. Even the apostle Paul was denied a healing three times.

You were created by God, so it shouldn't be hard to believe that He can fix what He made. We live in a sinful, broken world, but there are times between the moment of your birth and death that God might step in and heal. When He chooses to do so, it's His gift to you.

Prayer

Father, Your gracious love sometimes includes healing. I know that no one deserves this gift, but I thank You for the times You've cured me and the people I love. I know You can do it again.

Day 17
POWER TO HEAL [PART 2]

Read John 4:46–54

A certain royal official. . .heard that Jesus had arrived in Galilee from Judea, [and] he went to him and begged him to come and heal his son, who was close to death.

JOHN 4:46–47 NIV

Questions to Consider

- What signs and wonders has Jesus performed that have helped you to believe in Him?

- A nobleman heard Jesus say that his son would live, believed the word, then went on his way assured it was true. When have you heard Jesus' word, trusted Him, and went away assured of His truth? What miracle did you receive?

Today's Devotional

Jesus brought with Him a New Covenant. It was a divine contract that altered the terms of God's connection to mankind. His love was declared to all, and His rescue plan left no one without an opportunity to choose Him.

The people of Israel thought God's care was only for them. They acted as if every person who wasn't Jewish would always be on the outside looking in, no matter how much the outsiders wanted to know God.

The New Covenant? Well, it changed all that. It's important to note that as Jesus began His ministry His encounters with people who had been declared spiritual misfits increased. It was likely a surprise to many who witnessed the request of the outsider in John 4. This man had heard the stories about Jesus and thought it was the best opportunity to bring his dying son back to life.

Jesus doesn't just *say* He's for all. He proves it every single day.

Prayer

Thank You for allowing me to do more than look at Your plan, God. You have invited me in and given me a front-row seat to both Your plan and my purpose.

Day 18
LOVING THE UNLOVELY

Read Luke 5:12–26

*It came to pass, when he was in a certain city, behold a man
full of leprosy: who seeing Jesus fell on his face, and besought
him, saying, Lord, if thou wilt, thou canst make me clean.*

LUKE 5:12 KJV

Questions to Consider

- Have you ever fallen on your face and stated your faith,
  then simply and humbly awaited Jesus' response? How
  different is that from just telling Jesus what you want
  Him to do?

- What do you do and where do you go to recharge spiritually, physically, emotionally, and mentally?

- What do you do when the unlovely, unclean, and undesir-
  able approach you? Can you willingly reach out to them
  with the love of Jesus? If not, what might help you do so?

Today's Devotional

Have you ever thought you were too filthy for Jesus? You
did everything you could to try to clean yourself up first.
You wouldn't talk to Him and going to church seemed like
the last thing you should do. You might have reasoned, "If

God only knew the things I think and the things I've done He would change His mind about me." But He does know. And as with the leper in Luke 5:12, Jesus doesn't look away in disgust. You can go to Him in the rubble and ruin of your present condition, dropping all the shards of your sin and saying, "Lord, if You want to, You can make me clean."

Jesus wasn't appalled by the condition of the leprous man in front of Him. God is never appalled by the seeker in you. When you realize you need help—then ask for it—you can believe that the same God who healed lepers can cleanse you too. The promise of new life is for all who will ask.

Prayer

When I see myself as unlovable, Lord, I also see You as unapproachable. Thanks for teaching me that neither perspective is true. You love me. I can come to You. Help me to accept both as exceptional news.

Day 19
THE COST OF DISCIPLESHIP

Read Mark 8:34–9:1

[Jesus said], "If any of you wants to be my follower, you must give up your own way, take up your cross, and follow me."
MARK 8:34 NLT

Questions to Consider

- Do you truly want to follow Jesus or are you content to watch from a distance? Do you deny yourself or deny Him? Do you take up your cross or leave it behind?

- What do you think when Jesus says that if you want to save your life, you'll lose it—but if you lose your life for Him, you'll save it?

- Are you putting anything before God right now? What might you have gained lately at the expense of your soul?

Today's Devotional

Defining *discipleship* is pretty easy. This term applies to people who desire to know more about something and therefore learn all they can. You can be a disciple of sports, woodworking, or automotive trends. You might not think it sounds much different than being a fan, but discipleship goes a step further. You learn what you can and then you do something with what you know.

Being a disciple means you are no longer content to just know things *about* God. Instead, you choose to follow and behave in ways that demonstrate you're committed. If you don't actually follow God, it's very difficult to see what He's doing, celebrate blessings, or step in to help when He points out a need.

We follow God by following Jesus Christ. And true disciples follow wherever He leads. That means forsaking other desires, serving in areas you may have never imagined, or making big sacrifices. But for those who truly honor God, there are also big rewards.

Prayer

I don't want to treat You as just another interesting idea, Lord. I don't want to just follow You when it seems convenient. Help me to learn the value of trading my own way for Yours.

Day 20
WHO IS THE GREATEST?

Read Luke 9:46–62

*An argument started among the disciples as
to which of them would be the greatest.*
LUKE 9:46 NIV

Questions to Consider

- Are there any ways in which you are seeking to make a name for yourself rather than a name for Jesus?

- When was the last time you were determined to face something difficult? How might the things you're learning about Jesus help you face future challenges?

- What steps can you take to keep yourself looking forward instead of backward in your faith walk? What Bible verses might help you in this endeavor?

Today's Devotional

There are plenty of biblical warnings about comparing yourself with others. That's what the Pharisees did, and Jesus was repeatedly unimpressed. But that same "compare and contrast" mentality was showing up in His disciples.

They should have learned that His love was for all, His mercy was fresh each morning, and no one compared to

Him. They may have learned that but concluded that there must be someone among them who was *second*—which by extension meant that all the others were somehow worth less. Jesus had lived with these men, teaching them every day, and they wanted to reduce relationships to bragging rights.

In Luke 9:48 (NIV) Jesus settled their argument when He said, "It is the one who is least among you all who is the greatest." If the disciples didn't understand then, they would eventually. Jesus meant that if you regularly put others first, you'll ultimately stop caring if you're the greatest. And that is of great value in God's sight.

Men are naturally competitive, but Jesus wanted that competition to be transformed into compassion. People need to see God more than any human being. Be sure you're pointing others to Him, not yourself.

Prayer

Lord God, forgive me when I wonder if I am somehow more impressive to You than other people. This kind of thinking ended when Jesus taught about true greatness. It's an instruction I need to follow today.

Day 21
GREATNESS IN THE KINGDOM

Read Matthew 18

For the Son of man is come to save that which was lost.
MATTHEW 18:11 KJV

Questions to Consider

- Which verse in this chapter struck a chord with your heart? In what ways does that verse connect to, confirm, or address the present circumstances of your life?

- How does humbleness play a part in each of the vignettes presented in this chapter? In what ways does this make you stop and take stock of yourself?

- Who do you find yourself forgiving over and over again? Who do you need to forgive without reservation today?

Today's Devotional

Today's passage provides more clarity on the subject of who's the greatest. Tucked about a third of the way through the passage is Jesus' statement of purpose. He came to "save that which was lost." That is far greater than gold stars on a homework paper or participation trophies.

Sometimes people wonder what God thinks of them. When they do, they're forgetting that He thought so much of them that He sent His Son to pay the price for their sin. He promised forgiveness to repenting sinners and heaven to the rescued. That was Jesus' mission. It's what you needed, and it's what He came to do.

The question about who is Jesus' favorite seems petty. But it represents the way many people understand their world. Normal existence says there's a pecking order and someone must be at the top. *Of course* there will be employee of the month awards, popularity contests, and Fortune 500 lists.

But Jesus clearly didn't get that memo. He flatly rejects such things.

None of us are worthy of eternity with Christ. But praise God, He saves that which is lost. Jesus' life and death evened the playing field for us all.

Prayer

When I have You, Lord, what else do I need? You take care of me, love me, and give me purpose. You're more than enough.

Day 22
TRUE RICHES

Read Mark 10:13–34

[Jesus said], "I tell you the truth, anyone who doesn't receive the Kingdom of God like a child will never enter it."
MARK 10:15 NLT

Questions to Consider

- In what ways have you accepted Jesus and received the kingdom of God as a little child would? How can you maintain the total faith of a child?

- Where are your treasures these days—in heaven or on earth? What are they? In answering these questions, what insights are you discovering about your life?

- In what ways is God giving you the opportunity and motivation to put Him before all earthly treasures? How is He making what seems impossible, possible?

Today's Devotional

Have you ever been at a social event with other adults when children stepped in with questions and requests? Many grown-ups would cast furtive glances at the other adults and wonder when the kids will be shuffled outside. Children should be seen, not heard—or so the old mantra goes.

This might give you some idea of the way the disciples felt when kids wanted to spend time with Jesus. They considered these young'uns to be intruders. After all, Jesus had important things to say, and these children were interfering.

Well, that was the disciples' considered opinion. But Jesus disagreed. He enjoyed the kids' guileless attention. Many of the men who listened to Jesus undoubtedly had their minds on other things.

Children are a great example of faith. Their enthusiasm is visible, their questions unguarded, their joy contagious. Doesn't that sound like a great combination for the way you should approach Jesus?

Prayer

Lord, help me come to You like a child. I want our time together to be as memorable as a Christmas morning or a birthday celebration. May I never become "too old" or "too important" to be anything other than childlike with You.

Day 23
HEALING ON THE SABBATH

Read Luke 13:10–17

When Jesus saw her, he called her forward and said to her, "Woman, you are set free from your infirmity." Then he put his hands on her, and immediately she straightened up and praised God.

LUKE 13:12–13 NIV

Questions to Consider

- In what ways was Jesus a rebel? In what ways does He continue to be a rebel?

- What has weighed you down lately? What do you need in order to raise yourself up? What (or who) do you need in order to be straight?

- Are there any cases in which you're blindly following rules instead of the promptings of Jesus? What might He be leading you to do?

Today's Devotional

Jesus sometimes did things that made people think He was a rebel. This case happened on the Sabbath. The only thing people thought they were allowed to do on the Sabbath was worship God. But Jesus chose to heal a woman who was ill.

Shouldn't He have known better?

Critics overlooked the fact that Jesus is God. His actions suggest that people are more important than a specific day of the week. It would even seem that His help was an act of worship.

This must have been very hard for observers to accept. They had always been taught that any work on the Sabbath was forbidden, but Jesus *did* something on that special day. Condemning Him seemed an appropriate response. The religious leaders and others in the crowd felt justified in their condemnation. But Jesus restored health to someone who needed it. He showed love, which is one of God's greatest commands.

What seemed radical was just a simple statement—that doing good should be a part of every believer's daily experience.

Prayer

Lord, how I interact with others is important to You. Help me to remember that You've never forbidden Your people from blessings others, at any time or in any place.

Day 24
THE SIGN OF JONAH

Read Matthew 12:22–45

*[When answering the scribes and Pharisees, Jesus]
said unto them, An evil and adulterous generation
seeketh after a sign; and there shall no sign be
given to it, but the sign of the prophet Jonas.*
MATTHEW 12:39 KJV

Questions to Consider

- When you think of the "fruit" of your life, what is it revealing about you?

- How are your words justifying you? How might they be damning you? Should the fact that your words carry so much power change the way you speak?

- When have you asked God for a sign instead of relying on your faith? What prompted you to do so? What was the result?

Today's Devotional

Jesus was in town and people came out hoping for dinner and a show. The town must have been buzzing about the things He could do, and everyone wanted to see for themselves. They wanted to see miracles. They wanted Jesus to put on a performance.

What they received was something to think about—a miracle that didn't seem like a miracle at the time. He told the spiritual leaders who were present that an "evil generation" came out for the sole purpose of seeing a show. There would be no sign—just a reminder of a story they would remember. That story was the account of Jonah.

This Old Testament prophet spent three days in the belly of a big fish. Then he made a less-than-graceful exit onto shore, brushed himself off, and delivered the message God had commanded. That message—a sermon to the sinful city of Nineveh—resulted in the saving of life.

In a similar way, Jesus would be out of sight for three days, buried in the depth of the earth. Then He would leave His tomb to deliver a message that resulted in the saving of souls. The resurrection was certainly miraculous, but the vast majority of Jesus' followers through time never saw Him physically, either before or after death. For us, everything revolves around faith.

Prayer

I don't ever want to treat You as if You exist only to meet my needs, Lord. Help me to understand Your tasks and do what You ask without hesitation.

Day 25
THE ANOINTING AT BETHANY

Read Mark 14:1–11

*[Jesus said], "I tell you the truth, wherever the
Good News is preached throughout the world, this
woman's deed will be remembered and discussed."*

MARK 14:9 NLT

Questions to Consider

- When have you done all you could for Jesus? What more
  might He be prompting you to do for Him?

- When has Jesus nudged you to do something others
  scorned? Did you find yourself responding to His request
  or were you paralyzed by the naysayers? What was
  the result?

- How would Jesus want you to respond to critics—believers
  and non-believers alike—when you follow through with
  His leading?

Today's Devotional

A woman arrived at the dinner party Jesus attended. Everyone
watched as she took a very expensive bottle of perfume and
began to pour one drop after the other on Jesus' feet. She used
the perfume and her own hair to clean His feet from the day's

road dust. People began whispering behind their hands. They may have questioned the reputation of the woman, murmuring that she could have used water instead of perfume because of the cost. They might have even wondered if she was just showing off. It all seemed too. . .extravagant.

Jesus, who knows all things, also knew what His disciples were trying to keep quiet. In Mark 14:9, He made a promise. What this woman did would be remembered and discussed. And, all these centuries later, *you* are remembering and discussing her actions.

Is any gift for Jesus too elaborate? Is any sacrifice too great? Was there a limit on how much He loved You? Was His gift to You restricted or freely given? Do you think God cares most about you or is He more concerned about a spending limit?

Prayer

Lord God, You have given us the ultimate example of the lavish gift. Thank You for loving me so much. Help me to love You in return by serving You well. I know I do that by helping others.

Day 26
INSTITUTION OF THE LORD'S SUPPER

Read Mark 14:12–31

*While they were eating, Jesus took bread, and when
he had given thanks, he broke it and gave it to his
disciples, saying, "Take it; this is my body." Then
he took a cup, and when he had given thanks, he
gave it to them, and they all drank from it.*
MARK 14:22–23 NIV

Questions to Consider

- Does it increase your faith to know that Jesus is aware of everything you will face as you walk with Him?

- How can you prevent the communion ritual from becoming routine? What does the bread and wine really represent?

- Have you ever broken a solemn pledge to Jesus despite your determination to keep it? What does Jesus' restoration of Peter to an ever greater ministry tell you about your Savior?

Today's Devotional

Jesus gave the disciples an exceptional gift. He offered symbols that could be touched, tasted, and smelled as the long-lasting reminder of what He was about to do on the cross.

At the last supper, in a borrowed guest room in Jerusalem, the disciples probably didn't fully understand what was occurring. The unleavened bread (that is, made without yeast according to the ancient law) was passed from one man to the next. Jesus said it would help them remember His body which would soon be sacrificed for people's sin. The cup of the fruit of grapes, by its dark red color, reminded the men that Jesus' blood would be shed for humanity's rebellion against God.

Today we have a better understanding of what happened at the last supper. And while different traditions have varying views on what happens during the communion ritual today, we all see Christ's sacrifice as we partake. It is a powerful reminder of God's love for humanity through His Son, Jesus Christ. The perfectly innocent Man was betrayed, tried, convicted, and executed, taking our sins and punishment on Himself. He did what had to be done to rescue sinners. And you can enjoy the rewards of His labor.

Prayer

I am honored that You thought so much of me, God. Help me understand and appreciate Jesus' sacrifice every time I partake in communion. He did for me what no one else could. Remembering is a small but important gift that I can give.

Day 27
THE BETRAYAL AND ARREST OF JESUS

Read Luke 22:39–23:25

He that was called Judas, one of the twelve, went before them, and drew near unto Jesus to kiss him. But Jesus said unto him, Judas, betrayest thou the Son of man with a kiss?
LUKE 22:47–48 KJV

Questions to Consider

- How often do you follow Jesus at a distance? How might that affect how nonbelievers see you? How might it affect you?

- In what situations have you been as quiet as Jesus in these verses, knowing that's how God wanted you to be? When were you not able to contain yourself? What does Jesus' composure reveal about Him?

- When have you gone the way of the crowd instead of the way of God?

Today's Devotional

Adversaries can't betray you. They don't have your best interest in mind, so you don't expect loyal behavior. Betrayal can only come from the heart of someone you trust.

Jesus knew that Judas would betray Him. This was a

disciple who had been with Jesus throughout His ministry years. He agreed to follow when the Son of God asked. He heard the things Jesus said. In that respect He was no different than the rest of the twelve. The difference came in what Judas chose to believe. He witnessed miracles, experienced love, heard words of life. . .and yet betrayal bubbled up in his heart.

This betrayal was not an impulse decision. It was premeditated. Judas thought through his desire to betray Jesus and looked for an opportunity to earn money for it. He even created a signal—the kiss—that would alert authorities to the man they wanted to arrest.

Of course, Judas' plan was a bad one. But even at that, God could use it for His own good purposes. Judas ultimately felt a regret that led to his early death by his own hand. But the man Judas betrayed ushered in a new and everlasting life.

Prayer

I don't ever want to betray You, Lord, but I know I'm capable of anything. Help me to be a faithful friend and treat You with the honor and respect You absolutely deserve.

Day 28
THE DEATH OF JESUS

Read Matthew 27:33–56

Then Jesus shouted out again, and he released his spirit. At that moment the curtain in the sanctuary of the Temple was torn in two, from top to bottom. The earth shook, rocks split apart, and tombs opened.
MATTHEW 27:50–52 NLT

Questions to Consider

- How do you think Jesus, who possessed all power, felt about being presumed powerless? Have you ever had any similar experience?

- When have you been betrayed by a friend, or falsely accused, or unfairly cursed, and felt as if God had left you high and dry? Does it help to know Jesus suffered all that—and more—for you? Why or why not?

Today's Devotional

It can be easy to take the simple act of breathing for granted. In. . .out. . .repeat. Twenty-two thousand times a day—nearly 600 million breaths in the average life span. You don't even have to think about breathing. Our bodies actually work better when we breathe without giving it much thought.

Jesus pushed Himself up on the cross with His feet shackled and spiked. In. . .out. . .repeat. . .slump. He couldn't find any level of comfort as gravity made breathing a difficult event. In. . .out. . .repeat. . .shout. . .slump. When Jesus finally died many remarkable things took place. You read all about it in Matthew 27.

Jesus was 100 percent God and 100 percent human, and His sacrifice as a human redeemed mankind. His horrible end was your perfect beginning. But even His end was not the end of His story.

Prayer

Lord Jesus, it is uncomfortable thinking about You dying on a cross. But it happened, and it happened for a reason—God the Father's demand for payment for sin. Thank You for experiencing that horrible death so that I wouldn't have to.

Day 29
JESUS IS BURIED

Read John 19:28–42

Later, Joseph of Arimathea asked Pilate for the body of Jesus. Now Joseph was a disciple of Jesus, but secretly because he feared the Jewish leaders. With Pilate's permission, he came and took the body away. He was accompanied by Nicodemus.

JOHN 19:38–39 NIV

Questions to Consider

- Have you ever kept your faith in Jesus secret for fear of the reaction of others? Was it worth it? Why or why not?

- What do you think changed in Joseph and Nicodemus' lives to make them bold in caring for Jesus' body?

- Have you ever considered that the fall of humanity happened in a garden and that the rise of humanity also took place in a garden? What do such parallels tell you about God?

Today's Devotional

If death is a great darkness, then Jesus brought light—and life—to this dark place. His death? Confirmed. His body? Placed in a borrowed tomb. The world fell silent and some of those who witnessed His death wept. The Son of God who possessed the greatest wisdom the world had ever known had His voice temporarily silenced.

This in-between time was filled with fitful sleep for His followers, disillusionment among the faithful, and glee among the adversary's minions.

The disciples had thought they had a purpose—but when the one who led them was carried away broken and lifeless, they had no idea what to do with it. A group of soldiers guarded the tomb while the disciples hid, wondering if they would be next. This ending seemed like a betrayal of what they expected Jesus to do.

But hadn't He said He must die? Hadn't He said three days would pass and He would arise? Yes, He had—and Jesus, as "the truth," never lies. Though we often lose hope and despair, God's promises are always still in effect. Faith and time will prove everything we struggle to believe now.

Prayer

What a different story this would be if it ended here, God. But the story continued, because You had much more to accomplish. Please help me to remember that Your goodness is on the way.

Day 30
THE TOMB IS EMPTY

Read John 20:1–18

*Early on Sunday morning, while it was still dark,
Mary Magdalene came to the tomb and found that
the stone had been rolled away from the entrance.*

JOHN 20:1 NLT

Questions to Consider

- When was the last time you "ran" to Jesus? Where do you usually find Him?

- When have you seen and then believed? How are you blessed for believing in Jesus without having physically seen Him? What keeps your faith strong?

- What about God's Word is hard for you to understand? What about the Bible has Jesus made clear to you? What is He revealing to you now?

Today's Devotional

The stone that was rolled against the entrance to Jesus' tomb is thought to have weighed as much as four thousand pounds. Rolling it anywhere was much more than a one-man job. When Mary arrived she knew she would need help to get into the tomb. But she quickly saw that the heavy stone did not obstruct the entrance. Mary looked inside the grave, but did not see Jesus' body. This only added insult to the stress and uncertainty she had experienced over the previous week. Who would be so cruel as to steal the Lord's body?

Jesus had said He would rise from the dead. But His disciples had somehow overlooked, ignored, or blocked this promise from their memories. Jesus, though, never makes a promise He won't keep. When He said He would rise from the dead, He meant it—and rise He did.

At that moment death was defeated and the bridge between man and God was re-established. Because Jesus' tomb was empty, your life can be full. Because He rose from the dead, you will one day rise to eternal life.

Prayer

Lord, Jesus, when You rose from the dead You broke the power of death, brought freedom from the penalty of sin, and empowered me to follow You into eternity. Thank You! May I always respond to You with grateful obedience.

30 DAYS OF BIBLE READINGS FOR GROWING IN YOUR FAITH

It was by faith that Abraham obeyed when God called him to leave home and go to another land that God would give him as his inheritance. He went without knowing where he was going.
HEBREWS 11:8 NLT

A pumpkin will never approach world-record size if it only stays within the seed. In a sense, the pumpkin must die first in order to really live. After sprouting from the seed, the growing pumpkin needs to stay connected to its vine. It needs regular nourishment to become strong.

This is a picture of what it's like to grow in God. Die to self, live in Him, and the continuous connection to Him causes you to grow. When you truly want to go where He sends and do what He asks, you'll find yourself content.

Your third quest begins in the Word of God and continues there for the next thirty days. Grow in faith by immersing your soul in the living water of God's truth, allowing it to reach every available space.

Follow your reading with meditation—a time when you explore what you're learning. Take notes and revisit the quest at the end of this month. The goal is to become more godly, more like Christ, better able to handle the hardships of life and rise above them in faith. Are you ready? Let's go.

Day 1
FAITH: TRUSTING GOD WITH EVERYTHING

Read Genesis 22:1–14

Then God said, "Take your son, your only son, whom you love—Isaac—and go to the region of Moriah. Sacrifice him there as a burnt offering on a mountain I will show you."

GENESIS 22:2 NIV

Questions to Consider

- Can you think of a time you obeyed God without question or hesitation? What was at stake? How did that experience confirm and strengthen your faith?

- Has God ever provided *for* you as you made an offering He demanded *from* you? How did that strengthen your faith and trust in Him?

- What situation in your life is currently testing your faith and obedience? Will you need to sacrifice something to be fully faithful to God?

Today's Devotional

What if you asked God for something very specific and He gave it to you? What if, after you received what you requested, God asked you to give it back to Him? Would this seem fair? Would it seem right? Would you object?

Abraham received a promise from God. A son would be born to him in his old age. Abraham waited years for God to answer this promise. Then God asked Abraham to give up his son—by killing him. This seems extraordinarily harsh. It takes no notice of how long Abraham had to wait to enjoy his son Isaac. Yet, Abraham took the boy, walked to the mountain of God's choosing, and prepared an altar for sacrifice.

Once God saw that Abraham was willing to give up his son, God's messenger angel stopped him. God provided a substitute sacrifice and an old man walked home with his young son.

This story offers a parallel to the gift of God's Son. And while God spared the boy Isaac, He did not spare His own Son. This sacrifice—one that cost the Father dearly—was the means He used to rescue you. That's how much God loves you.

Prayer

I will likely never face what Abraham did, Father. But when You ask me to give something up, help me to trust that You have a good plan. I want to honor You with my obedience.

Day 2
FAITH: TRUSTING GOD THROUGH PRAYER

Read 1 Samuel 1:7–20

*[Hannah] vowed a vow, and said, O LORD of hosts, if
thou wilt indeed look on the affliction of thine handmaid,
and remember me, and not forget thine handmaid, but
wilt give unto thine handmaid a man child, then I
will give him unto the LORD all the days of his life.*

1 SAMUEL 1:11 KJV

Questions to Consider

- Have you ever gone to the Lord with brokenness, pouring out your soul to Him in prayer? What happened next?

- What vows have you made to God? How faithful have you been to your promises?

- How do you approach God in prayer—from the heart or from the head? What is the difference?

Today's Devotional

Hannah was brokenhearted. Soul exposed, she asked God for what she wanted. And she asked. And she asked again. Hannah even vowed to God that if He gave her the son she longed for, she would give the boy back to the Lord's service.

God sent an answer. A baby named Samuel filled his

mama's heart with joy. Would Hannah be faithful to her promise? Yes. The boy she had prayed for grew up to be "the prophet Samuel" who anointed kings and led the nation spiritually. Hannah had seen the miracle of a promise and understood the value of obedience.

Many of us have come to expect that when God makes a promise He will keep it (He's never broken one yet). But what about our own promises, whether to God or to our families and friends? Keeping vows may cost more than you planned, but your word should be sacred. Be careful in making promises, but when you do, be sure to fulfill them.

Prayer

Lord, I have come to expect that You will keep Your vows. It's comforting to know that You will do what You say. Please help me be as serious about my own vows.

Day 3
FAITH: TRUSTING GOD FOR PROTECTION

Read 2 Chronicles 20:20–30

The king appointed singers to walk ahead of the army, singing to the LORD and praising him for his holy splendor. This is what they sang: "Give thanks to the LORD; his faithful love endures forever!"

2 CHRONICLES 20:21 NLT

Questions to Consider

- How often, in difficult circumstances, do you find yourself looking around instead of up? What can you do to keep your eyes focused on God?

- When have you sung praise to God in the midst of a seemingly hopeless or potentially dangerous situation? Did that outlook help the situation?

- What can you sing praise to God about today?

Today's Devotional

King Jehoshaphat wanted his nation's enemies to leave his people alone. He adopted an unusual military strategy. Most people wouldn't think of bringing in singers for the sole purpose of honoring God—and then making this unusual entourage the front-line soldiers. It wasn't what anyone expected, but God responded. "At the very moment they began to sing and give praise, the LORD caused the armies of Ammon, Moab, and Mount Seir to start fighting among themselves" (verse 22 NLT).

What those enemy armies squabbled about is less important than knowing that God did mighty things for the people who were sold out to following Him.

How did God follow up this victory that started in praise? Verse 26 (NLT) says the people "gathered in the Valley of Blessing, which got its name that day because the people praised and thanked the LORD there."

As an encore, God did one more thing. "Jehoshaphat's kingdom was at peace, for his God had given him rest on every side" (verse 30 NLT). What might God do with your praise?

Prayer

It is good to give thanks, God, and to remember that Your faithful love never ends. You walk before me on my very worst days and never leave me when things are going well. Simply knowing You gives me reason to praise.

Day 4
FAITH: TRUSTING GOD TO THE END

Read Daniel 3

*The king's command was so urgent and the furnace so
hot that the flames of the fire killed the soldiers who
took up Shadrach, Meshach and Abednego, and these
three men, firmly tied, fell into the blazing furnace.*
DANIEL 3:22–23 NIV

Questions to Consider

- Have you ever worshipped something—a person, thing, or idea—more than God? What came of this misdirected faith?

- When have you declared faith and trust in God regardless of whether He saved you from trouble? How did that situation go?

- When have you been "unsinged" by a difficult spiritual, physical, emotional, or financial circumstance? How does that history encourage your faith walk?

Today's Devotional

God created you for worship—and you will worship. That's part of God's law. Even if it weren't, though, people inevitably worship something or someone. It may not be God, but human hearts will hold up something as an object of love and desire.

Some of us have saved up money to buy what we worship, spent more time with it than we should have, and couldn't find time to think about much else. It's not right, but it's also nothing new.

Nebuchadnezzar, king of ancient Babylon, understood the importance of worship. He just got the *object* of worship wrong. Nebuchadnezzar demanded people worship something other than God. When three young men from Israel said no, the king lost it. He used a furnace to execute the uncooperative men. But God would not let His guys burn.

These men knew that God was the only proper object of worship. Even if Nebuchadnezzar succeeded in killing them, they would die with a clear conscience. But Shadrach, Meshach, and Abednego didn't die that day because God rescued them. And by their example, the king himself learned something important. He ended the day honoring the God who rescued the righteous.

Prayer

Lord, teach me the value of right worship. Bend my knee to Yourself, and make my heart Yours alone. If my attention drifts, in Your great mercy bring me back to Yourself.

Day 5
FAITH IN HIS POWER

Read Matthew 8:1–13; 15:21–28

Then Jesus answered and said unto her, O woman, great is thy faith: be it unto thee even as thou wilt. And her daughter was made whole from that very hour.
MATTHEW 15:28 KJV

Questions to Consider

- When have you seen Jesus' healing touch reaching beyond time and distance?

- How persistent are you in prayer for the healing of loved ones? Has that process changed you in any way?

- Do you tend to tell Jesus how you'd like Him to heal you? Or is it enough to know that He *has* the power to heal? What role does faith play when you either receive what you pray for—or don't?

Today's Devotional

How powerful is God? The Trinity—God the Father, Jesus the Son, and the Holy Spirit—is the ultimate, absolute power in the universe. That seems like an obvious answer, but you might still wonder what it really means.

The earth, moon, stars, sun—and everything else in

space—were all in a day's work for God. But He created and maintains the microscopic world as well, holding atoms and molecules together in things both inanimate and living. This same God wired your mind, heart, and soul to want to know Him.

In Jesus' time, it was God's power that healed the sick and raised the dead. Throughout time, He has supplied air, water, and food for His creation. He makes the rules and offers forgiveness when people break them. You couldn't do one-millionth of the things that God can. So why does it seem easy to disregard Him, the God who gives us everything we need to live?

God offers His power because He's the only one who can. He meets human needs on a second-by-second basis. Ideally, His power should inspire within us a quiet and sincere "thank You."

Prayer

There is power in Your name, Lord. There is power in prayer. There is power in Your Word. Help me to rely on Your name—through prayer—by Your Word.

Day 6
FAITH IN HIS TOUCH

Read Matthew 9:18–31; 14:34–36

Jesus asked them, "Do you believe I can make you see?"
"Yes, Lord," they told him, "we do." Then he touched their
eyes and said, "Because of your faith, it will happen."
MATTHEW 9:28–29 NLT

Questions to Consider

- When has your persistent, determined faith to reach out and touch Jesus made you well—spiritually, physically, emotionally, or mentally?

- Why is faith so important to receiving what we ask from God? How has your faith developed over time?

- What "touch" do you need from Jesus today?

Today's Devotional

When you request His help and Jesus gets involved in your struggle, things will change for the better. For believers, His divine touch is at times comforting, healing, and correcting.

This touch can be the reassurance you need, the hope you thought was gone, or the guidance that leads you away from being lost. It is just what you need, more than you expect, and it inspires a desire to keep experiencing it.

Jesus' touch is tied to the relationship God—the all-powerful Trinity—has with you. Jesus is like a friend draping His arm over your shoulder, telling you things are going to be alright. Sometimes He offers a restraining touch, redirecting you to better things. Sometimes He's shaking your hand or slapping your back, indicating that you're making progress. Jesus' touch will always meet you in your place of need.

Prayer

Lord, I don't feel Your physical touch like some people could two thousand years ago. But I know You are always with me, urging me on to better things. Please make me aware of Your presence and influence—Your touch—in my life.

Day 7
FAITH IN ACTION

Read Matthew 17:14–20; 21:18–22

[Jesus said], "Truly I tell you, if you have faith
as small as a mustard seed, you can say to this
mountain, 'Move from here to there,' and it will
move. Nothing will be impossible for you."
MATTHEW 17:20 NIV

Questions to Consider

- When have your needs driven you to your knees before Jesus? What remedy did you request? What part did your faith play?

- How has Jesus' promise that "with God all things are possible" (Matthew 19:26) affected your prayers?

- In what areas of your life do doubts erode your faith? What can you do to change that?

Today's Devotional

When was the last time you expressed faith and then saw tangible evidence of what your faith believed? It's easy to pray, asking God for help, then act as if the help is never coming. Chances are good that your prayers will be ineffective until you truly believe God can and will help. The biblical pattern is pray (persistently) then wait (expectantly) for God to act.

Many people seem to think their requests are courtesy calls or some type of spiritual obligation before they begin the real work of figuring things out for themselves. And sometimes we do work out our difficulties to some conclusion—but we've likely sidestepped the perfect answer.

If God can take bad circumstances and create good outcomes why would we ever invite Him into our struggles and then refuse His help? Ever done that? We all have. But let's commit to doing better. Some general feeling that God exists won't help us at all. God grants faith. We need faith. Faith moves mountains. So exercise your faith and wait for Him to act.

Prayer

*When I pray, Lord, keep me from treating
prayer as just something on my to-do list before
I figure things out for myself. Remind me that
You can and will help based on my faith.*

Day 8
FAITH GROWS

Read Isaiah 40:27–31; Mark 10:13–16

*They that wait upon the Lord shall renew their strength;
they shall mount up with wings as eagles; they shall run,
and not be weary; and they shall walk, and not faint.*
Isaiah 40:31 kjv

Questions to Consider

- In what ways do you nourish your faith so that it grows beyond things that are easy to believe? What role do God the Father, Jesus, and the Holy Spirit play in your spiritual advancement?

- How do you wait on the Lord with confidence and hopeful expectation? Have you ever seen this increase a strength you didn't realize you had?

- Why do you think scripture includes stories of Jesus welcoming little children? Can you imagine yourself as God's child? What does that imply for your relationship to Him?

Today's Devotional

If you are hang gliding for the first time, that last step off a cliff will cause some anxiety. If you're learning to ride a motorcycle, lifting your foot from the pavement can create a moment of fear. The same is true for water skiing, cliff rappelling, and virtually any activity that relies on skills you haven't yet developed. You're surrendering your body to experiences that seem unnatural.

God wants your faith to grow, and you need it to grow. It may seem safer to define faith as something that leads you to church every weekend. But that view stops short of the adventure that renews strength, decreases weariness, and provides the ability to keep walking with God.

If you want your faith to grow, bring along your expectations, patience, and gratitude. Then challenge God, asking Him to move what seem like mountains to you. He can. Do you believe?

Prayer

It's so easy to stick with what I know, Father. Please help me to take that frightening step out into the unknown. I know that You will always be with me.

Day 9
FAITH IN GOD'S GLORY

Read John 7:38–39; 20:24–31

"Anyone who believes in me may come and drink! For the Scriptures declare, 'Rivers of living water will flow from his heart.'" (When he said "living water," he was speaking of the Spirit, who would be given to everyone believing in him. But the Spirit had not yet been given, because Jesus had not yet entered into his glory.)
JOHN 7:38–39 NLT

Questions to Consider

- Through Jesus, God provides supernatural water for spiritually parched people. In what ways do you thirst for God? How do you satisfy that thirst?

- How have you allow God's Spirit to refresh others through you?

- In what areas of life do you give more credibility to what you can see rather than what you believe? How might Jesus be prompting you to believe and be blessed?

Today's Devotional

Spend time focused on God. This might seem like an obvious statement. But it needs to be said. Why? Well, most people will focus on the *idea* of God without really getting to know Him. This kind of thinking makes God a concept and bypasses His companionship.

If you truly believe in God, you'll actively show up to consume the living water He offers. By your faith in Jesus, through the Holy Spirit, God's life is lived out through yours.

God is awesome. This, too, seems like an obvious statement. But it needs to be said. Why? Because your faith is stronger when you are immersed in Him. Don't just stay at the water's edge enjoying the beauty of the stream. Wade in, dive deep, and satisfy your spiritual thirst. Get involved! The Christian life isn't a spectator sport.

Prayer

I want to know You, God. I want to dive into Your deep, refreshing living water and enjoy every possible benefit of my relationship with You. Then use me to bless others.

Day 10
FAITH IS INTENTIONAL

Read Romans 10:17–21; 2 Corinthians 5:6–7

Faith comes from hearing the message, and the message is heard through the word about Christ.
ROMANS 10:17 NIV

Questions to Consider

- How are you hearing the "word about Christ"? How has hearing the message increased your faith?

- When has God held out His hands to you? How did you recognize His outreach in your life?

- How might your life change and your faith grow if you intentionally sought God's presence? How can you actively listen for His truth?

Today's Devotional

Faith isn't a virus that you catch. It's not a bacteria that grows without your knowing it. It isn't some childhood disease that passes. Faith happens because you hear what God says and then you respond. Faith is a choice and an intentional pursuit.

You don't receive faith as a gift from a friend or family member. If you don't want it, you don't have it. Faith is never forced on you but it is certainly offered to you. It's the starting point of every God quest.

God has been seeking you your entire life. Of course, He always knew where you were and everything about you—but He waits for you to recognize Him. You aren't a Christian because you have a Bible, attend a church, or listen to Christian music. You aren't a Christian because you work for one, live by one, or have a family member who is one. You're a Christian if you've been intentional about listening to the word of Christ and responding appropriately.

This faith will change your life for the better. And all the more as it grows.

Prayer

Lord, I want real faith. Help me to listen and respond to what You say. I want to believe what I can, then ask You for faith to believe even more.

Day 11
FAITH THROUGH YOUR DOUBTS

Read Galatians 3:1–14

How foolish can you be? After starting your new lives in the Spirit, why are you now trying to become perfect by your own human effort?
GALATIANS 3:3 NLT

Questions to Consider

- Do you attempt to please God through the things you do? Or do you spend time in His Word and prayer, seeking the filling of His Spirit? Which do you think is most appealing to God? Why?

- How do you keep the gospel fresh in your mind? How can the good news of Jesus ward off spiritual doubts?

- How well do you rely on God and step out in faith for an uncertain future? How can you do even better?

Today's Devotional

Have you made your faith about you? It's easy to do. In fact it's common. Most people want to arrive at the place where they ease God's burden by no longer requesting His help.

You might subscribe to an "I got this, God" philosophy. He's given you new life. He knows what you ought to do.

He knows how to help you. But you stop recognizing His leading and venture out on your own again—how well do you think that will work out?

Galatians 3:3 calls this game plan foolish. "Human effort," in the apostle Paul's phrasing, won't get you anywhere in God's eyes. Having accepted God's rescue through Jesus, you don't automatically know what to do, how you should do it, and when you've done enough. You must stay connected to the vine, as Jesus said (John 15:5).

Your best human effort is the reason Jesus had to die. Your best effort will never improve on its own. Accept the help that only God can provide.

Prayer

*It doesn't matter why I refuse Your help, Father—
it's always wrong for me to try to live apart from
You. Remind me that Your help is essential—
it's the only way to develop this new life.*

Day 12
FAITH DESPITE THE FIGHT

Read Philippians 3:7–11

I consider everything a loss because of the surpassing worth of knowing Christ Jesus my Lord, for whose sake I have lost all things. I consider them garbage, that I may gain Christ.

PHILIPPIANS 3:8 NIV

Questions to Consider

- What aspect of your life has become less important as you have advanced in your faith walk? What has become more important?

- Do you think you're better at following rules or knowing Christ? Why?

- What would it be like to know Jesus so well that you experience His resurrection power? How close are you to doing so?

Today's Devotional

That promotion at work? Rubbish. The award you received last year? Toss it in the trash can. The raise you worked hard for? Not worth the paper it's printed on. As men, we often think differently—all of these things are very important to us! But when compared to Jesus they are, in fact, worthless.

His life coursing through your own, by faith, leads you to a place you'd never find by yourself. It's a gift you could never afford. It's a wonderful life that never ends.

When you meet Jesus face-to-face and He wipes away your tears, your pain will be banished—forever. At that point, do you think you'll want to talk about your hard work, the raise, the award? Or will the things that seemed so important be exposed as trivial when compared the gift of eternal life? Remember, that's yours because of something you never did.

Faith recognizes garbage when it sees it. The more time you spend with God, the more you'll see the difference between your own tiny accomplishments and the absolutely life-changing achievement of Jesus.

Prayer

*Lord Jesus, help me to want You above all other
things—to know You and love You and enjoy You.
The achievements of my life are nothing, Lord.
I thank You for giving me true meaning.*

Day 13
FAITH TO APPROACH GOD

Read Hebrews 4:16; 10:19–25

Let us therefore come boldly unto the throne of grace, that we may obtain mercy, and find grace to help in time of need.
HEBREWS 4:16 KJV

Questions to Consider

- How bold do you feel in approaching God in prayer? Why?

- Knowing that Jesus experienced all the trials of human life, are you more or less inclined to approach Him for help? Why?

- What makes you presentable to God? Why is Jesus' sacrifice so important to your spiritual success?

Today's Devotional

Many men lack skills in the "total honesty" category. We like to pretend we know what we're doing, and we find it hard to acknowledge that we might have messed up. The motto seems to be, "Fake it till you make it."

If only we were as bold in approaching God as we are in trying to convince people we have it all together. Maybe we'll fool some of the people, some of the time. But we can't really fool ourselves, and we certainly aren't fooling God.

So let's just admit it. We don't know everything, we can't fix everything, and we'll never figure out everything on our own. It's refreshing to be honest, isn't it? Jesus, who does know everything, can fix everything, and never needs to figure things out—because He already knows everything—can help with every need we have. And He's made a wide-open way for us to approach God the Father.

Step up, speak your peace, and make sure God knows you want Him to act on your behalf. You can't do it alone, so why even try?

Prayer

I want to be bold with You, Lord, trusting in Your wisdom and strength rather than my own. May I come to You, the first time every time, for the help I need.

Day 14
FAITH IN OUR FUTURE HOME

Read Hebrews 11

They were looking for a better place, a heavenly homeland. That is why God is not ashamed to be called their God, for he has prepared a city for them.
HEBREWS 11:16 NLT

Questions to Consider

- As creator of all, God spoke visible things out of nothing. In what ways does His Word continue to fashion your world?

- How does the Hebrews 11 "Faith Hall of Fame" encourage your faith? Which characters do you most identify with?

- How does the faith of martyrs and heavily persecuted people affect your own faith? Why would they hold so tightly to Jesus in spite of such trials?

Today's Devotional

"In the beginning," God created our earth. "In the end," we'll live with Him in a better place, as today's scripture indicates. "In between," where we live now, we personally suffer and we ache for others who suffer. It's a hard world, so faith in our future home is vital to our mental and spiritual well-being.

The heroes of Hebrews 11 were good, but not perfect. They did many things right—starting with trusting God. They could overcome their own fears and doubts and passions as they kept their eyes on Him and His "heavenly homeland."

Whoever wrote Hebrews notes that these faith heroes "died still believing what God had promised them. They did not receive what was promised, but they saw it all from a distance and welcomed it. They agreed that they were foreigners and nomads here on earth" (11:13 NLT).

We are foreigners and nomads as well. If you ever feel like you don't belong in this world, you don't. This is a temporary phase of life, on your way to perfection in God's presence. Like those biblical heroes, keep looking ahead. Keep the faith in your future home.

Prayer

Lord, I know the struggles of this life. I can only imagine the joys of the next. Thank You for saving me through Jesus. Please strengthen my faith in the future home He's preparing for me.

Day 15
FAITH DRIVES GOOD WORKS

Read James 2:14–26

Faith by itself, if it is not accompanied by action, is dead.
JAMES 2:17 NIV

Questions to Consider

- What good works does your faith prompt you to perform? How well do you obey those urgings to do good works?

- Who can you help today? What actions can you take to alleviate another person's suffering, either directly or indirectly, openly or anonymously?

- How are your actions—your works—making your faith complete? How are your works showing others that God is changing you?

Today's Devotional

Faith is a matter of giving God your problems and allowing Him to do what only He can. But it is not an excuse to sit back and live without purpose.

You can and should do what God prompts you to do. He will use your hands, feet, and voice to accomplish great things. His plan fulfills His purpose, and He uses people like you who are willing to help.

You might hear that a friend has a very specific need. You pray for that friend, send him a text wishing him well, and think about him from time to time. What if you had the very thing he needed? You might have been thinking that God could miraculously supply the need without your help. . .but He might be watching to see if you could be His answer to prayer.

Works cannot save you. But they provide evidence that the change you'd love to see in others is a change that's happening within you.

Faith without works is simply telling God you *won't* help. Don't ever pass up an opportunity to do a good deed. It honors God, helps you, and blesses others. It proves your faith is real.

Prayer

Lord, please help me to exercise the faith You've given me. Remind me to pray for needs and to step in with assistance when it's within my power to do so.

Day 16
FAITH IN THE SPIRIT

Read John 15:26–16:15; 1 John 3:21–24

He that keepeth his commandments dwelleth in him,
and he in him. And hereby we know that he abideth
in us, by the Spirit which he hath given us.
1 JOHN 3:24 KJV

Questions to Consider

- How often do you think of the Holy Spirit's presence and work in your life? Why?

- How is the Holy Spirit guiding you? What truths is He revealing to you?

- Which of the Holy Spirit's roles—Comforter, Counselor, Strengthener, Advocate, Intercessor—do you sense most powerfully in your life right now?

Today's Devotional

God doesn't give His Spirit to people who have not agreed to walk with Him. You won't find counsel, godly comfort, spiritual strength, or a God who prays for you without the Holy Spirit. You'll need the Spirit to lead you on God's perfect path. Without Him, you'll either wander aimlessly or take some easier path that leads away from God.

Your faith in God comes with the gift of the Holy Spirit, but you might not think of Him often. Some hardly think of Him at all. But the Spirit always thinks of you, and He is guiding you this very moment.

Have you ever noticed that you are making different decisions than you made before you were a Christian—or even from the time when you were young in the faith? The influence of God's Spirit on your decision-making is evidence that a "new you" is being worked out, one day, decision, and promise at a time.

You should be learning from God's Spirit. Are you? What truth are you considering today that you weren't before? There are potent discoveries to be made when God's Spirit speaks into your life through your spirit. He can, and will, change your thinking for the better.

Prayer

Lord, I can do natural things on my own. But to do spiritual things I need help. Thank You for giving me the companionship, guidance, and power of Your Spirit.

Day 17
FAITH IN THE FINAL OUTCOME

Read 1 John 5:1–12

Who can win this battle against the world? Only those who believe that Jesus is the Son of God.

1 JOHN 5:5 NLT

Questions to Consider

- When did you gain eternal life through Jesus Christ? How has your life changed since that time?

- How is your faith in Jesus Christ providing spiritual victory now?

- How does your perspective change when you realize that, because of your faith in Jesus, you are already living the forever life?

Today's Devotional

If you've ever been to a gym, you may have seen motivational posters that encourage you to believe you are a winner. But we know that these affirmations don't have any inherent power. Sure, positive thinking can add a spark to your motivation, but it cannot sustain you to the end the way Jesus can.

Even as a Christian, you will need to battle the world, the flesh, and the devil. And sometimes you will fall short, coming up on the losing end. But when God looks at you, He sees the finished work of Christ. You *are* a winner. Not because of anything you do but because of what God has already done. Jesus Christ has achieved your forgiveness and He offers it freely. Jesus defeated death on the cross, and eternal life waits for those who will take hold of it. You win because the perfection of Jesus is applied to your spiritual account.

You are a winner for one reason and one reason only—Jesus loves you. Know this, internalize it, and accept it. God's Word confirms it. Lives have been changed by it, and hope has been restored because of it. It truly is good news.

Prayer

Lord Jesus, You won my victory on the cross. I don't have to be defeated by sin or fearful of death. May I live every day by faith in Your goodness and power, not my own ability.

Day 18
OBEDIENCE TO HIS COMMANDMENTS

Read 1 John 2:3–6; 2 John 6–9

If anyone obeys his word, love for God is truly made complete in them. This is how we know we are in him: Whoever claims to live in him must live as Jesus did.

1 JOHN 2:5–6 NIV

Questions to Consider

- Who do you think Jesus may have found difficult to love? Who do *you* find difficult to love? In what ways can you love that person with the love of Jesus?

- How does loving others and walking like Jesus grow your faith? How does it demonstrate your love for Him?

- Why is faithfulness to the teachings of Christ so important? What does it mean if we fall away from Jesus' teaching?

Today's Devotional

In your family there was likely an expectation of obedience. If your parents told you to do something, they didn't want to hear you say, "You know, it's great that you're taking care of me. The food is good and my room is appreciated. . .but well, I just don't feel like working today."

This response doesn't show appreciation. Sure, you could

say it in a pleasant way, but you're indicating that obedience is not on your agenda. This is what God lives with every day. People like His gifts, but they don't want to do what He says. It even seems like they're happy to accept the good stuff He offers but they'd survive just fine if He walked away. That isn't the kind of relationship God had in mind.

He knows everything—which means He knows what you need to get to the place where you should be. He gave you directions, and the logical course of action is to go where He leads—not to stay where you are or try your own way or listen to someone else who refuses to obey.

The Bible does more than offer us comforting passages to read. It's a plan that can lead us to an exceptional life. But only if we choose to obey.

Prayer

Help me see Your Word as life instruction, God. May I never view Your commands as simply suggestions or helpful hints.

Day 19
OBEDIENCE TRUMPS SACRIFICE

Read 1 Samuel 15:12–23

*Samuel said, Hath the LORD as great delight in
burnt offerings and sacrifices, as in obeying the
voice of the LORD? Behold, to obey is better than
sacrifice, and to hearken than the fat of rams.*
1 SAMUEL 15:22 KJV

Questions to Consider

- Have you ever prided yourself on following God's leading
  only to later realize you'd fallen short of what He wanted
  you to do?

- Why might you only hear part of what God says? What
  can you do to ensure you're giving God your total attention
  and entire obedience?

- In what areas of life do you need to obey and submit to
  God today?

Today's Devotional

God said to go out and win a battle. King Saul said he would.
God gave him instructions, but King Saul ignored most of
them. God used the prophet Samuel to confront the king
and Saul pulled out a list of excuses.

Have you ever had a similar encounter with God? Most of us have. We're not alone in the struggle to obey Him.

In Old Testament times, people would offer sacrificial animals as a way of paying for their sin. God had told Saul he shouldn't bring anything back from his battle, because everything was to be destroyed. But Saul kept the best of the enemy's livestock. When Samuel asked him about it, Saul said something like, "Oh, ummm, these? Yeah, I just, you know, thought they would be a great sacrifice to, ummm, God."

Of course, these animals were the spoils of war and not even from Saul's own herds. If he really considered these animals as sacrifices, Saul would experience no personal loss from giving up what he didn't really own.

But that's not even the primary issue. God wasn't interested in sacrifices from Saul. The Lord wanted the king's obedience. Saul did things his own way, and paid a heavy price.

Prayer

Lord God, sometimes I presume upon Your forgiveness and mercy. Instead, I should obey You, immediately and wholeheartedly. Please make my heart less like Saul's.

Day 20
OBEDIENCE HONORS HIS HOLINESS

Read Psalm 119:1–10

*As I learn your righteous regulations, I will
thank you by living as I should! I will obey
your decrees. Please don't give up on me!*
PSALM 119:7–8 NLT

Questions to Consider

- How does submission to God's will, Word, and way result in your joy and God's pleasure?

- How can you keep your whole heart seeking after God? What can you do to keep your spiritual appetite strong and nourished?

- When might you have felt you were far from where God wants you to be? What in God's Word inspires you to keep following Him, to celebrate milestones of faith?

Today's Devotional

When you hear that God is sinless does it seem logical to celebrate by saying, "To honor Him I will be the exact opposite of what He is!" That's probably not something you would say. But perhaps your actions speak the same message loud and clear.

How would your life look if you absolutely and without reservation believed and said the words of Psalm 119:7–8? Here's a paraphrase for you: "Your Word teaches all kinds of truth, God. Your instructions lead to right living. I am grateful, so I will live the way You want me to. Will You help me? I will obey each instruction. And when I fail, don't give up on me."

God is holy. He is completely distinct from His creation. Set apart. Sinless. These differences should cause you to want to be more like Him—not less. They should cause you to recognize that His way is better—not worse. They should make you long to be holy and set apart—not someone who looks a lot like he did before meeting the Lord.

God's "righteous regulations" are plainly stated in His Word. Our obedience to them honors His holiness.

Prayer

There are a lot of things I'm not, Father. Help me to become ever more like You because my choices reflect Your instructions.

Day 21
OBEDIENCE LEADS TO RIGHTEOUSNESS

Read Deuteronomy 6; Romans 2:1–16

*It is not those who hear the law who are
righteous in God's sight, but it is those who obey
the law who will be declared righteous.*
ROMANS 2:13 NIV

Questions to Consider

- In what ways does obeying God's commands and worshipping only Him keep you in a figurative "land flowing with milk and honey"?

- How does recalling all God has done for you keep your faith strong and your walk sure?

Today's Devotional

You hear things every day. Some thoughts are rejected immediately, some are considered and then cast aside, and a few are judged valid and kept. This last set of ideas cause you to change your beliefs. They alter the essence of who you are and give you a new direction to follow.

This isn't like listening to a safety message while waiting for takeoff in an airliner. You don't really have to pay attention or change your habits to fly in a jet—you just have to endure the speech.

But God says it's not enough to just *hear* the truth about Him. You will need to do something more—that something is obedience.

To be clear, you gain salvation only by faith in Jesus Christ. But once you're covered by His sacrifice, God wants you to follow His holy laws, which before only pointed out your failures. Accepting Christ makes you righteous in one sense; your choice to obey God's rules builds on that righteousness and honors God.

Prayer

You call me to obey, God. It has always been my choice, but I miss out on blessings when I ignore what You say. Please help me to do what You say.

Day 22
OBEDIENCE, BECAUSE OF DELIVERANCE

Read Joshua 22:1–5; Romans 6:17–18

*Take diligent heed to do the commandment and the law,
which Moses the servant of the LORD charged you, to love
the LORD your God, and to walk in all his ways, and to
keep his commandments, and to cleave unto him, and to
serve him with all your heart and with all your soul.*

JOSHUA 22:5 KJV

Questions to Consider

- When have you left something behind in order to focus more fully on God? How did God reward you for that sacrifice?

- How do people love and serve God with all their heart and soul? What does that phrasing imply about our obedience?

- When have you felt like a servant to sin? Do you consider yourself a servant to righteousness? Why or why not?

Today's Devotional

God is not your copilot. If you're going to go anywhere good, it's because He's the leader and you have chosen to follow Him.

Christians are "delivered" individuals. Sin was the defining characteristic of your past, but it no longer should define your future. It can describe your present, but that's not what God desires for His sons. Sin could also define the future—but only if you live in constant rebellion against the God who provides deliverance.

Do you think God rescued you so you could walk back into your spiritual prison and slam the cell door shut? Who would do that? Sadly, some people do—every Christian who lives with the fear of what he might give up by following God.

Yes, you'll have to leave some things behind when you start to follow Christ. Some of those things even feel good—for a while. But the more you know of God and the Christian life, the more clearly you see how destructive those old behaviors and attitudes are.

Now that you've been delivered, don't revisit the mess of your failed past. There are so many reasons—good and perfect ones—to say out of the prison.

Prayer

I want to walk where You lead, Lord. I want to go where You send me. I want to follow because every step with You is further from all that's been wrong in my life.

Day 23
OBEDIENCE TO THE ONE WHO SUSTAINS

Read John 15:1–17

[Jesus said] "Remain in me, and I will remain in you. For a branch cannot produce fruit if it is severed from the vine, and you cannot be fruitful unless you remain in me."

JOHN 15:4 NLT

Questions to Consider

- What steps do you take daily to "remain" in Jesus, as a branch connected to the vine?

- How does Jesus sustain you, physically, emotionally, and spiritually? What have you seen Him provide in ways both miraculous and mundane?

- Knowing that Jesus chose *you* to rescue, love, and live in, what can you do to love Him in return?

Today's Devotional

Pull an immature grape from the vine. You can probably guess that the grape will stop growing. It will not reach maturity. It will start to decay.

Plants are one example Jesus used to let His disciples know the truth about growth—or the lack thereof. Plants are intended to grow and so are men of God. It was not His plan to leave you without the resources you need for growth. Yes, you are weak. There are moments when you're not sure you can face the various circumstances that are stacked against you. There are moments when insecurity suggests you are unworthy to accept God's gifts. There are moments when you believe you are the worst sinner in the world. Each of these moments works to separate you from the vine that supplies the nutrition you need for spiritual life and health.

Recognize your position in Christ, as an accepted and cherished son of God. And obey the Son by "remaining" in Him. You can't grow on your own. And you don't have to.

Prayer

I want to stay connected to You, Lord. I want to grow in You and with You. Please nourish me in ways that make me useful in Your plan.

Day 24
OBEDIENCE BRINGS STRENGTH

Read Luke 6:46–49; Acts 4:18–21

Then [the religious leaders] called them in again and commanded them not to speak or teach at all in the name of Jesus. But Peter and John replied, "Which is right in God's eyes: to listen to you, or to him? You be the judges!"
ACTS 4:18–19 NIV

Questions to Consider

- How is your faith strengthened when you go to Jesus, listen to His teaching, and obey Him?

- In what areas of your life might you be calling Jesus "Lord" but not following through with what He wants you to do?

- Have you ever stood against the crowd in following Jesus? How did it feel in the moment? How did God respond?

Today's Devotional

Some people resist calling Jesus "Lord." Why? Well the term may imply a boss, an employer, or some other "greater than." Some men don't want to say *Lord* because it seems to lower their own status. They don't really want anyone telling them what to do.

In Acts 4, Peter and John were detained by the Jewish

religious leaders. These men wanted the disciples to stop talking about Jesus. News of this intriguing rabbi was only growing stronger after His death and resurrection. The leaders were still trying to tamp down the impact of the man they had killed. They certainly had no intention of calling Jesus "Lord," believing Him, or walking in His steps. The religious leaders were doing an excellent job of keeping a bad choice moving in an equally bad direction.

But by their choice to follow Jesus ("boss," "greater than," "*Lord*"), Peter and John could grow in strength despite opposition. Might there be something to learn from their choice to call Jesus "Lord"?

Prayer

*On my own, Lord, my authority is limited and
so is my influence. But when You are Lord in
my life I grow in strength and impact. Today,
I bend my knee and call you Lord!*

Day 25
OBEDIENCE TO TRUTH

Read Psalm 1; Acts 5:28–32

Blessed is the man that walketh not in the counsel of the ungodly, nor standeth in the way of sinners, nor sitteth in the seat of the scornful. But his delight is in the law of the LORD; and in his law doth he meditate day and night.
PSALM 1:1–2 KJV

Questions to Consider

- What would happen if you made it your daily ambition to seek treasures of truth from God's Word? What wealth have you discovered already today?

- How would meditating on the truth of God's Word and obeying what you find nourish and prosper your life?

- Does knowing that you have the Holy Spirit, the originator of all truth, living within you make you more confident? Why or why not?

Today's Devotional

One of the biggest arguments of the moment is whether absolute truth exists. Can there be a truth that is applicable at all times and in all situations? Or do circumstances change the truth itself? Should you stop believing what God says simply because someone in leadership suggests it may not be true? There are all kinds of people saying that, you know.

But the people saying such things are missing one very important thing—God Himself. As a Christian, however, you know Him, and you know how wise and trustworthy He is. So always fall back on God's opinion, as you find it in the words of scripture. Obey what God Himself says, not what some "thought leader" may think.

Let's make this as simple as possible: If anyone suggests you believe anything that goes against God's Word, go with God. . .every time.

Prayer

Lord God, You have said You will bless me when I choose Your Word above the people who mock You. Establish me in Your great work and give me the courage to obey.

Day 26
OBEDIENCE WITHOUT QUESTION

Read Genesis 12:1–4; Deuteronomy 11:1–15

"You must love the LORD your God and always obey his requirements, decrees, regulations, and commands."
DEUTERONOMY 11:1 NLT

Questions to Consider

- Have you ever been like Abram, stepping out in faith and obeying without question, not knowing where God was leading you? How does God bless such obedience?

- Where might God be calling you to step out now? What obstacles threatened to sidetrack you from walking in faith?

- How confident are you that God will take care of you in every circumstance because you obeyed Him? Why?

Today's Devotional

When God says "Go!" do you say, "Why?" When He asks you to obey, do you ask, "What's in it for me?" When God gives you an assignment, do you complain?

You might have reservations about obeying God without question. But the Bible is filled with stories of men who obeyed and left questioning God out of their decision-making.

You'd be amazed to see what life could be like if you obeyed God the first time, every time.

You don't have to know the *why* to know the *who* behind the command. Children are safer when they learn the voice of their parents and respond immediately when they hear that voice. Imagine a boy wanting to run across the road to the park: he's not paying attention, and there's an oncoming car. Dad calls out, "Stop!" Now, the boy has a choice to make, and it's going to be life-altering. He can obey immediately, though it seems that by doing so he'll miss out on the fun of the park. Or he can disregard the command, and perhaps lose his life.

Obedience spares that boy from disaster. It can do the same for us. We may never know what trouble we avoid by doing what God says. But He does.

Listen for God's voice. Trust His commands. Obey without question.

Prayer

Lord, this issue of obedience can reveal the selfishness deep inside me. Give me strength to resist my own inclinations in favor of the things You know are best for me.

Day 27
OBEDIENCE YIELDS BLESSINGS

Read Leviticus 26:1–13; Psalm
119:56–62; James 2:10–13

You are my portion, LORD; I have promised to obey
your words. I have sought your face with all my heart;
be gracious to me according to your promise.
PSALM 119:57–58 NIV

Questions to Consider

- What blessings have you experienced by your worship of God and obedience to His will?

- How would you describe your spiritual walk lately? Have there been any detours from God's path? What changes would benefit your current faith journey?

- Are there any "little sins" in your life that threaten to cause bigger problems?

Today's Devotional

Many guys settle for a life that looks for loopholes in God's Word. They try to find ways to satisfy sin's sweet tooth while still being okay with God. It's a form of dancing on the edge of a cliff, of inching closer and closer to some place outside God's will.

Trying to get away with as much as you can doesn't indicate a heart-quest to follow God. Sadly, this has been true of men for generations. All of us have moments when we embrace the loophole.

If God is all you need (and He is), make a promise to obey His commands. Then keep that promise. Seek God's face and discover mercy in what God has committed to you.

Asking forgiveness doesn't have to be our default setting. Certainly, when you sin, confess it and accept forgiveness. But by the power of God's Spirit, the act of obedience can be your first and regular response. Playing with fire, just struggling to get along, is not a choice that leads to thriving.

Blessings await your arrival at the place called Obedience. Set your course and go.

Prayer

Lord God, I have been guilty of rationalizing poor choices. Remind me that I don't ever need to rationalize obedience. Your rules make me a better man. And I never need to be ashamed of doing right.

Day 28
OBEDIENCE MATTERS

Read Ezekiel 5:7–8; John 14:12–24

Jesus answered and said unto him, If a man love me, he will keep my words: and my Father will love him, and we will come unto him, and make our abode with him.
JOHN 14:23 KJV

Questions to Consider

- When has your disobedience to God resulted in a less-than-ideal outcome?

- Consider a time when you felt a lack of harmony between yourself and God. How did He ultimately break through to you? What did you need to do to restore fellowship?

- How does the Holy Spirit help you follow Jesus' words and teachings?

Today's Devotional

When you choose to disobey God you are saying a couple of things. First, you are suggesting (quite clearly) that you are more interested in your own way. Second, you are saying you'd prefer that God stay out of your business. At some level, conscious or otherwise, you're saying that God shouldn't decide what's good for you.

We've all seen movies, or read stories, or even observed cases in real life of overbearing parents. Their children feel oppressed and become angry with extreme commands that really don't benefit the child. But that's not the way God treats His children. God is wise and loving, not overbearing and oppressive. His commands are beneficial for His children, even if they don't fully grasp that truth in the moment.

Read His Word and discover a God who loves humanity and works for its ultimate benefit. In fact He's doing that in your life right now. This is just one more reason obedience matters more than you think.

Prayer

Lord, I never want to think of You as oppressive. Please give me a heart that trusts You with the best outcomes. I want to follow You without hesitation or reservation.

Day 29
GROWTH THROUGH HIS PROMISES

Read Jeremiah 11:3–5; 2 Peter 1:3–8

*Because of his glory and excellence, he has given us
great and precious promises. These are the promises
that enable you to share his divine nature and escape
the world's corruption caused by human desires.*

2 PETER 1:4 NLT

Questions to Consider

- What are you hearing God speak into your life today?
  How are you obeying (or disobeying)?

- What promises have you seen God deliver? If He hasn't
  seemed to fulfill promises, why do you think that's the case?

- How do God's promises grow your faith?

Today's Devotional

We should all experience a powerful personal revelation in
2 Peter 1:4. It's easy to accept the general idea that God has
made promises and delivers on every one of them. But this
verse makes an impressive claim: as God keeps His promises,
you experience His divine nature working in your life.

What's more? All the corruption and human desires that
dwell in your own heart are negated by God's escape clause.

That doesn't mean you'll be perfect, but it does mean the grip of sin on your life won't be absolute. Obedience to God is possible. It means you can reject any idea that you have no choice when temptation comes.

And if you inch back one verse, there is more good news. Second Peter 1:3 (NLT) says, "By his divine power, God has given us everything we need for living a godly life." You see, there is never a reason to say that the Christian life is impossible. God gives you everything you need to succeed. It's a promise.

Prayer

Lord, I thank You for the gifts that leave me without excuse. Your promises give me the motivation and the power to live a life of obedience.

Day 30
GROWTH THROUGH HIS LIKENESS

Read Ephesians 5:1; Philippians 1:27; 1 Peter 1:13–22

*As obedient children, do not conform to the evil desires
you had when you lived in ignorance. But just as he
who called you is holy, so be holy in all you do.*
1 PETER 1:14–15 NIV

Questions to Consider

- God wants you to imitate Him, following in His footsteps, like Father, like son. In what ways is His resemblance growing in you?

- What aspect of your old self tries to call you back into your former life? What aspect of your new self calls you forward into God's life?

- How has your love for God, yourself, and others changed during this study?

Today's Devotional

You are a special tool on God's workbench, to be used for a very specific purpose. You are a special, set apart instrument of His blessing. You were made in God's likeness, for His purpose, and for this particular time.

So why allow yourself to be used for things God never

intended? He recognizes that men can live that way in ignorance, which is why He gave us His Word. That's where we learn how He makes godly men.

Your acceptance of salvation through Jesus allowed you to discover a new life. God broke the chains that held you in sin and sorrow, and put you onto a path of freedom and joy. All the while, the Holy Spirit transforms you as You submit to Him.

The all-powerful Trinity is ready and willing to make you into a new creation, a new-and-improved man far better than you once were. Work with God, and He will complete the job He's started in your life. Obey Him, and grow into His likeness.

Prayer

I have so much to learn, Lord, but You are a great teacher. Give me ears to hear You and a heart to obey. I thank You for changing my life for the better.

ANOTHER GREAT RESOURCE FOR MEN

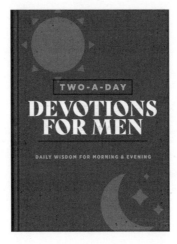

You'll enjoy these concise readings, two for each day of the year, to inform your mind, lift your spirit, and challenge your behavior—all in pursuit of becoming more like Jesus Christ. Written by men, for men, these meditations touch on a wide range of topics relevant to Christian living.

Printed Hardback / 978-1-63609-554-7